Burning Bushes & Moon Walks

Burning Bushes & Moon Walks

Calvin Miller

WORD BOOKS, Publisher
Waco, Texas

Contents

1. The Incendiary Moment   7

2. Christ and War   17

3. Of Monks and Ministers   30

4. The Hucksters   39

5. The Great Contemporary   51

6. The Proper Cause   61

7. Space Faith   73

8. The Citian: A Study of Anonymous Man   85

9. The Straight Man in a Bent World   95

1

The Incendiary Moment

In Christ we are offered the possibility of partaking in the reality of God and the reality of the world, but not in the one without the other.

Dietrich Bonhoeffer
Ethics

FOUR DAYS following the inauguration of President Kennedy, an American strategic bomber crashed near Goldsboro, North Carolina. Aboard the bomber and therefore among the wreckage were two 24-megaton nuclear devices. The bombs carried on routine security flights were protected from accidental detonation by a series of triggers which had to be tripped in sequence to release the fire-storm the weapons held within them. When the bombs were located, it was discovered that five of the six triggering devices had already been tripped in one of them.

The weapon, lying there in its "near-destruct" phase, with an unaware nation quite near the fuse, is symbolic of our nervous times. The moments are not all fiery, but they are all inflammable. Most current issues seem ready for easy ignition, whether or not they ever burn. We are pinched threateningly between future and past into an uncomfortable moment of action or pain we cannot leave.

The *now* has never been a long moment but it has always been ugly. The future holds promises and the past holds reminiscences, but the *now* is stark and tangled and often incoherent in its demands. Fortunately, we are not alone in the *now*, for it is the only place where God can live too. He does not lurk ahead of us in the *yet* nor does he enjoy reading history, but we are locked together with him in the ever-moving moment.

It is strange that we have so often visualized him as the God of yesterdays who is really so unfamiliar with the world. And we still have him there, Lord of the past, in his Bronze Age trappings, giving out his commandments to turbaned bedouins. Our minds seem to fold him into ancient history much faster than they will see him a contemporary. Although we never permit ourselves the admission, we feel that we would be more likely to see God on an old Renaissance canvas than the Staten Island ferry.

He fits the *then* better than he fits the *now*, or so it seems. Maybe it is his name, Jehovah. The name just sounds like the God of Moses more than it does the God of John Doe. But the name of God, Jehovah, is really thought to stem from the Hebrew verb *to be* in its present tense. It may have come from the word meaning *I am*, a great name for the *now* God.

God first disclosed his name, Jehovah, when an Egyptian-in-exile, Moses, stood at a burning bush, and God said, "I am who I am." His name was the present moment of time. He could scarcely have gotten Moses' attention by claiming to be a "Great Was"! Moses did not need a "has-been" God, but an "is." As a shepherd he had already come to know God's prowess in creation. What God had done was magnificent, a real conversation piece. But nobody really had time for talk.

The *now*, however, was where his countrymen, unpaid and overworked brickmakers, were. Moses could not afford a God who was afraid of knotted social issues. If redemption was possible, it had to be in the incendiary and dangerous present. If Moses was to make God's emancipation proclamation, it had to be simple and backed by a show of force—immediate and convincing.

"Let my people go!" said Moses, "or deal with the I-Am God." But Raamses was intractable as he encountered the Immediate God. So the *I Am* acted with swarms of flies and frogs, bloody rivers, hail, fire, darkness and an eerie plague of death that struck in every home, not excepting the palace. But freedom grew, and liberty was born out of slavery because the *now* God acted in the only place he can act: the ugly and fiery present.

The *now* in which God proved himself Raamses' contemporary has been gone 3400 years, and we find ourselves at the current *now*. It is the more serious than all the *nows* which went before it because it is our hopeless and unmanageable moment.

It is filled with the cries of millions of starving people. Its war is eating youth in a vain attempt to feed a lavish, expanding appetite. It has forced us to attend the exhibitionisms of its sex revolution whose neo-decency we have unwarily traded for many of the arts. Our children are becoming men very early and rioting in social tantrums. Space beckons. Inflation threatens. Psychology warns us about our pace. The nuclear armaments race has put a new tremor in the earth's already wobbly spinnings.

There is plenty of redeeming that could be done, but we seem to be fresh out of burning bushes and *now* power. Man has been playing redeemer (a role in which he is clumsy and for which he is ill fitted) in most of the crises of the day. Most of the efforts are ending in assassinations, counter-assassinations, and political debate. Every issue is explosive. Every promise is utopian. Nearly every cause is messianic.

The *now* is not only volatile and crammed with demanding social issues that will not be ignored, it is a world everywhere changing. We feel uncomfortable in a universe where our every thought must be updated and nothing that we touch is quite what it was when we touched it yesterday.

But God is the God of change. The great principle of conversion is the principle of change and renewal. And once the Christian has become a new person, he cannot tolerate an old and decadent system of any sort. He has become new and he wants the whole world that way.

The words *now* and *new* have more than a semantic similarity. When God encounters the moment, something comes into being that had not been before. God exerts force on the bent moment to make it straight again. Conversion is this unbending, this remaking.

Redemption begins in a man's contempt for his spiritual status. He despises self and wants it renewed. So in the *now*-disgust, he brings himself into encounter with God, and straightening occurs. Once he is straight, he can have no more respect for his bent world than he once had for his bent self. He is impatient for social redemption.

The charge of being two-faced has been leveled at many Christians because they have turned their backs on human interrelations. Having undergone the transforming power of the *I Am*, they seem to have lost interest in it. The world has demanded, "How can Christians care so earnestly that God transforms man, but not men? Can the God who redeems a man not redeem society?"

This has become the most glaring sin of evangelicals in our time. In love with fervent traditions and warm clichés, we have ignored the needs of an insurgent humanity. We have gone "soul-chasing" with marked New Testaments, while larger conglomerations of human beings have been searching for "soul" in riots, bread-lines, and militant reform. The search for a social soul has been the most burning drive of our time and the most fruitless. The irony of the world, folding over on itself in vacant and haunting nihilism, has arrived. "Jesus saves!" seems to hold nothing hopeful beyond its evangelistic milieu: He does not always save from employment injustices, nor social and racial inequalities.

Some evangelicals have accepted responsibility for making disciples, and that is important. But many have not yet accepted any responsibility for the world. Without saying it they have never accepted the universe as a part of the arena in which they must live and struggle. Margaret Fuller is once said to have stated: "I accept the universe!" To which Thomas Carlyle reportedly responded, "By God, she'd better." To the Christian unwilling to accept the universe and his redeeming responsibility in it, we can say as did Carlyle, "We had better accept it while it is yet here."

Of the few evangelicals who have heard God's voice in the volatile *now*, most are merely "thinking it over" as their substitute for action. William Barclay has it:

> Often when we say, "I'll think about it," all that we really mean is that we don't want to decide. Very often the phrase is just an evasion, an excuse for inaction. . . . I think that we ought to be very careful that when we say, "I'll think about it," we don't in fact mean precisely the opposite.[1]

Usually when evangelicals say "I'll think about it," we do mean just the opposite; we are going to see to it that the thought never protrudes into consciousness again.

We manage to avoid the demanding *now* by always looking to the future or contemplating the past, living between utopia and the "good old" days. The Israelites, having been redeemed from bondage, rarely ever caught sight of the moment and its requirements. They too either longed for the good old days when they were back in Egypt with "the leeks, the onions, and the garlic" or the future bliss they would enjoy in the land that "flows with milk and honey" (Num. 11:5, 13:27). We just as often seek asylum in the future and the past. When the painful moment comes that we are forced to look at the present with its knotted problems, we often say "I'll think about it."

Sometimes I wonder if what we mean by the good old days is that life was simpler, God less necessary, and spiritual obligations unknown. If that is what we mean then we must say again, "There have been no good old days." God has always required a world consciousness and concern.

The Book of Jonah is the saga of a man who tried to skip

out on his world consciousness because he had a racial bias. That solution did not work and never does. Nor would we be wise to attempt to skip out on our world responsibility.

This was part of our Savior's last command in Matthew 28:19–20. He has asked us to go into all the world, "teaching them to observe all things whatsoever I have commanded you." Evangelical interpretation of this passage sees it entirely as a command to make disciples. The meaning can scarcely be correct with so narrow a definition. The "all things" which Christ commanded must be his teachings on social responsibility and world welfare. To give to the poor, to abandon retaliation, to care for the widows and orphans, to deny self, to lay down our lives for our brethren, to feed the world's hungry, to heal the world's diseases: all are his commands. We dare not take "all things, whatsoever I have commanded you" and pretend that Jesus meant only the winning of men's souls.

In Matthew 25:31–46, there is a picture of the last judgment. Those who are condemned to hell in the passage are so condemned because they had no sense of obligation to their world. Of their own admission, they had ignored starvation, disease, poverty, and imprisonment, and Jesus was forced to say to them, "When you ignored your world responsibility, you ignored me too" (or words to that effect).

Jesus' half-brother James was critical of early Christians who claimed to have faith but no social concern. To James the practice of caring in the present moment was the Christian faith; he felt, too, that caring and faith were interdependent (James 2:14ff.).

The current apathy may point up the real problem. We have been guilty of religiosity without faith. Being religious and having faith are not the same thing; in fact, they are really antithetical. Gabriel Vahanian, though wrong about the death of God, may be right in his analysis of faith and religion. "Just as death is the loss of being, so religiosity is loss of faith in God. Death constantly threatens existence, as religiosity threatens faith in God." [2]

We are religious. We may have assumed, therefore, that we have faith and world concern. In reality we are a calloused people living in an exposed world.

Reports of human indifference to human need are frequent these days—man's inhumanity to man, as the cliché runs. Persons have been mauled and beaten before the very eyes of seemingly disinterested witnesses. Few seem to care about even the injustice to which they are witness. Nobody wants to get involved. The risk that is always present in involvement may be the very reason that Christians have turned their back on the bandaged times.

In the capitol city of New York, a youth who had been an inmate in one of the state's mental institutions stood for two hours on a twelfth-story ledge, incapable of making a decision to kill himself. While he teetered in his uncertainty, a crowd of four thousand people gathered on the sidewalks below him. Sick in mind, the man had to listen as the crowd below him began to jeer and yell obscenities, while spotlights played on his haunting, desperate face. Human concern was missing from the pitiful pageant. "Jump!" yelled one voice. "What are you waiting for, *Chicken?*" Then someone began taking bets: "Five to one he doesn't jump!" Someone else, afraid of missing the grisly event, said, "I sure hope he jumps on my side."

There is a sad and savage sadism about unconcern in a crisis, but flippancy in the face of desperation is hell-deserving. While it is true that present disciples have infrequently mocked the world estate, they have also infrequently cared. And the result of social apathy has been an erosion of confidence in the value of the gospel.

The church must discover and accept its responsibility to the Good News. But before it can begin its social evangelization it must grasp securely two things: the incarnation and Christ as servant. The Good News is but an austere philosophical façade without them.

Jesus claimed that he was the incarnation of God. The idea seemed preposterous! That God could live in a human form, or indeed that he would, was not hastily accepted. Still, a few believed that in truth "God was in Christ"! They did so not because Christ claimed to be the incarnation, but because they, ordinary men, observed the incarnation. What he did corroborated splendidly what he said.

He spoke of God's love and then went out to the lepers. He scooped up armfuls of children and then talked about the Fatherhood of God. He went into a Samaritan village and then spoke of a God who excluded none on the globe from his providence. His service to God preceded his sermons about God; he practiced the Kingdom of God first and preached it later. He was God, and it was obvious to some.

"Let this mind be in you which was also in Christ Jesus," said Paul of Tarsus. Simply put, "Become an incarnation of Christ!" We must let service precede sermons. We must let the bent people know that churchmen are not just orators, but God-possessed and Christ-inhabited. We must assault the bent people visually with our incarnation of him, otherwise they will not believe.

We have made our sound, and they have discovered it is sound alone. They have heard the Good News, and the hearing has not saved them. They are waiting to see the incarnate churchmen winding their ways into orphanages to love the children, and see them reading to blind men. They want to see them demanding parks for the high-rise ghettos, and teaching their children the dignity of every being and the death of discrimination.

Incarnation always means condescension, not in the sense of a patronizing relationship, but an equalizing one. Like Christ we must find a leprosarium and like him we must go into it or the people there will not believe. Like Michael Hamilton we must learn condescension, and we must not only learn it but we must love it.

I myself learn the doctrine of the Incarnation: that in order to minister to people you have to come down or up to where they are, not to get shocked or surprised at what they

are or do, but to start with them from where they are and
not where you might like them to be. God did not shout
down advice to us humans over the ramparts of Heaven,
but rather came down and shared our problems.[3]

Whether or not we can learn condescension in time to save
a world that has about decided it does not want to be saved
remains to be seen. But we must not assume that in our
inability or unwillingness to be the incarnation of Christ, we
can simply shout down its people. They have heard our
polemics about the bleeding world, now they have to know if
we can handle the bandages and tourniquets. We have taught
our first-aid long enough. Can we leave the lectern and work
in the disaster area?

Sadly enough, our failures will be costly indeed. For if
they do not accept us as the incarnation of Christ, neither will
they accept Christ as the incarnation of God. Only when they
see Christ living in men will they accept the thesis that God
was in Christ. They will not believe either one until the
church has learned as much about foot-washing as it knows
about fund-raising, administration, and promotion.

The church, through us, must take the role of the servant.
Christ expects us to, for he reminded us that the servant is
not above his Lord. With Paul, later disciples must call
themselves *douloi Christi*, servants of Christ. Harvey Cox
has reminded us that the church is to be the *diakonos*, deacon
of the city, the servant to technopolis. The church must become the world servant and it must do it now.

The *now*, as we have pointed out, is where God lives and
acts. He and his universe are on the move and will not stand
still while we meet in worship, important as that is. In this
moment and in every moment which preceded it, the world
needs redeeming, but it must be redeemed on the run. It is
moving. God is moving. It is time for the church to move
too.

Roger Shinn wrote a parable which encapsulates the *now*
God:

There was a time in the Old Testament history when men wanted to build a temple for God. But God said no. He preferred to live in a tent, for He was a God on the move, a God not bound to place. As time passed and society changed, God consented—so His people believe—to the building of a temple. . . .

If today men build to His glory, they will use the steel and stone, the glass and plastics of modern society, not the animal skins of ancient tents. But they will know that their building and all their human institutions are fragile and temporary. The God of history is on the move. A people who serve Him will be a people on the move.[4]

God is moving. And the evangelicals must match his pace.

We have cared too narrowly. Quickly, we must ask God to broaden our concept of redemption, until "Jesus saves" means a salvaging of human hope and an active love for all in need, anxiety and despair.

When we have arrived at a bigger definition of redemption and have begun to demonstrate that we really do care, then those who distrust our emotional and selfish shibboleths will hear us and society will have found its soul at the burning bush. Then too, Christians, long silent, will have gained a voice in the volatile *now* and we may honestly invite men:

> Come with us to Christ.
> Love broadly.
> Act responsibly.

2 *Christk and War*

The Master, watching Western Christendom today, with all our hatred, bitterness, war, would have to say, If this is Christianity, then I am not a Christian.

Harry Emerson Fosdick
Christianity and Progress

CHRIST CAME to the world at the precise time when every loyal Jew was looking for him. But he did not come in the manner in which the Messiah-seekers were expecting him. They were looking for a "rod out of Jesse," a knight in David's blood line, a charismatic warrior to call the nation to insurgency, revolution, and ultimate victory. Instead he came a baby, a helpless, whimpering infant. A general they would have hailed; the baby they ignored.

It was not that the infant's countrymen did not want peace. They wanted it; but they wanted it on Jewish terms, accompanied by a new Jewish respect, and perhaps accompanied by smug satisfaction that their ancient grudges against the gentiles had been sated. God would thereby make known his deep affection for Semites and his tolerance of lesser loved races.

Several pressing questions plague the Christ student of our day: Did this God-in-an-infant-Jesus in any way fulfill the warrior role? What did Jesus say about war? Was he a militarist or a pacifist or either? Did he believe in limited war? Would he support a just war? "Would Jesus carry a draft card?" These are difficult questions to answer.

The angels of the nativity sang, "Peace on earth to men of good will!" The implications of this Christmas anthem are that the infant Jesus in some way was about to usher in an eternal cease-fire. It is difficult to harmonize the rapture of the angels with the statement made by the mature Jesus: "Think not that I am come to send peace on earth; I am not come to send peace, but a sword" (Matt. 10:34). So we are confronted with a conspicuous credibility gap. Whom do we believe—Jesus or the angels? The angels had come from God with the message so they ought to have had it straight. If Jesus did come to cause war, then we have no other conclusion than that the angels must have sung their anthem of peace with their fingers crossed, and winked their jesting to the shepherds between stanzas.

One might wish that the angels had it right, for the fact is that between 500 B.C. and A.D. 1924 there have been 967 major wars between states. Very infrequently have there been periods of twenty-five years or more when there was not a military campaign in progress. Even our own country has been involved in nine major wars since the American Revolution—which is one conflict every quarter of a century. The cost of war in money and lives has soared beyond belief. World War I cost the United States 25 billion dollars, and a world total of 8 million soldiers' lives were lost. World War II cost the United States over 323 billion dollars, and all enemy and Allied troops killed were 19,500,000.[1]

As grim as these statistics are, they would be dwarfed by any real military confrontation among today's nuclear powers. The casualty statistics could equal two-thirds of the current census of either or both of the countries involved in such a conflict. Most people have imagined the possibility of such a war but have managed to submerge it beneath the immediate and the routine. But underneath the active and the conscious

it remains, threatening and ominous. Joseph Sittler pictured
the problem correctly:

> The substance is this: Annihilating power is in nervous
> and passionate hands. The stuff is really there to incinerate
> the earth—and the certainty that it will not be used is not
> there.
> Nor have we an anodyne to hush it up or power to run
> away from it. We can go skiing with it, trot off to Ber-
> muda with it, push it down under accelerated occupation
> with the daily round, pour bourbon over it, or say our
> prayers—each according to his tactic and disposition. But
> it goes along, survives, talks back.[2]

We have lived with it, but we do not like it. It is like going
to sleep each night with the certainty that Dr. Frankenstein
is in the basement and we may never see the light of the new
day. War is now ultimate, and Jesus seems too long ago and
far away to help us much. But if he has anything to say to
us we should desperately like to know it.

First of all, we must deal with his pledge to send a sword
upon the earth. Jesus was under no illusions as to the future
strength of his influence in a bellicose world. It was not that
Jesus doubted the ability of his Father's love to end all conflict; God's love was armed with reconciliation for single
citizens or entire nations—but man was the incompetent.

In his Sermon on the Mount, Jesus said, "Ye have heard
that it hath been said, Thou shalt love thy neighbor and hate
thine enemy; but I say unto you, Love your enemies, bless
them that curse you" (Matt. 5:43–44). So the specific sin
which causes war is hatred—our inability to love our enemies.
This sin is the antecedent to war in nearly every situation.

Man cannot cease sinning, and only in rare cases is he able
to curb his hatred and resentments for others. As long as one
man can hate another, one nation can build missile pits
sheathing another's destruction. If two men can allow their
pride and arrogance to flare into a fight, two nations can
deploy armaments to destroy each other.

It would seem that the nations of the West who have had

centuries of catechism and Christian practice would be the
most able to put into practice Jesus' command to love their
enemies and bless their censors. But even these Western
nations whose confession is nominally Christian seem unable
to practice Jesus' wisdom and love.

Here's the rub. The recent world wars have proved once
again that war is a possibility, even between Christian nations. Germany, Britain, France, America, Italy, and Russia
were all Christian nations, or at least nations with a long
tradition of the Christian religion and a strong established
church. Yet these nations, most of whose soldiers had been
baptized as infants, declared an international bloodfest of an
extended duration. In such wars, on both sides there are men
with firm commitments to Christ firing on each other, and in
some cases wounding and killing.

When Christians face each other across the trenches, they
have reached the height of the warfare dilemma. Each of
them is owned by Christ and employed by opposing governments. Christ says that they are to love their brethren and
fellow disciples whatever their uniform. Their political over-
lords have paid them and trained them to wipe out anyone in
a certain color of uniform whatever his religious convictions.
So they must face the issue of the supreme allegiance—Christ
or their homeland; Jesus or Caesar.

As former pastor of a military congregation, I was asked
most frequently by servicemen: "Is my military career in
harmony with the teachings of Jesus?" The question comes
without a tailored answer. But it grows out of a feeling of
schism within the person, a split within the personality of
anyone who tries to give his fullest allegiance to two antitheses. Although in peace the antitheses are submerged in
bivouac and routine training and typewriter infantries, in
war the issues jump quickly to life; and the Christian soldier
in the trenches looks hard in search of a warm rationalism
that will keep his eye steady in the gunsights. Even the
Christ-adoring infantryman who believes in the democratic
state he is defending may be torn in heart trying to figure out
how Jesus would have slung his M-16 in a jungle trench.

A young man who presumably hated Communism and was serving in Vietnam in the United States Army wrote back home:

Dear Mom and Dad:

Today we went on a mission and I'm not very proud of myself, my friends, or my country. We burned every hut in sight.

When the 10 helicopters landed this morning in the midst of these huts, six men jumped out of each chopper and we were firing the moment we hit the ground. We fired into all the huts we could. Then we got "on the line" and swept the area.

It is then that we burn these huts and take all men old enough to carry a weapon. The choppers come and get them (they take them to a collection point a few miles away for interrogation). . . .

So everyone is crying, begging and praying that we don't separate them and take their husbands and fathers, sons and grandfathers. The women wail and moan. Then they watch in terror as we burn their homes, personal possessions, and food. Yes, we burn all rice and shoot all livestock.

Some of the guys are so careless! Today a buddy of mine called, "La dai" ("come here") into a hut and an old man came out of the bomb shelter. My buddy told the old man to get away from the hut, and since we have to move quickly on a sweep, just threw a hand grenade into the shelter.

As he pulled the pin the old man got excited and started jabbering and running toward my buddy and the hut. A GI, not understanding, stopped the old man with a football tackle just as my buddy threw the grenade into the shelter.

After he threw it (during the few seconds delay) we all heard a baby crying from inside the shelter! . . .

After the explosion we found the mother, two children and an almost born baby.[3]

We are inclined to brush aside the conflict which may arise partly out of the naïveté and sensitivity of the young soldier and his fledgling understanding of the dangers inherent in Communism. Still, any such event as the one he described would, or at least should, awaken the conflicting loyalties to God and the state.

Every action of the disciple who follows Christ, in or out

of war, must be consistent with his Christ-image. It is this
Christ-image which determines the character of the disciple.
One must admit that it is difficult indeed to imagine Christ
taking part in such carnage. Would he give such utter loyalty
to any political system that he would act in total disregard of
human life?

Jesus appears in most New Testament passages as an
ardent anti-militarist. In Matthew 4:8 he refused Satan's
offer of the emperorship of the world, presumably because
the title and prestige lay on the backside of war and armed
conflict. In Matthew 5:39 he encouraged cheek-turning as
an obvious gesture of conciliation rather than retaliation. In
a subsequent verse (v. 41) he taught that if anyone (presumably a soldier who might conscript a grudging Jew to
carry his baggage) forced a man to go a mile, he ought to
demonstrate a conciliatory spirit and go two. When Peter
drew his sword (Matt. 26:52), he said, "Put up again thy
sword into his place; for all they that take the sword shall
perish with the sword."

Conversely, however, there are passages which suggest
the opposite conclusion. For instance, Jesus suggested that
men render unto Caesar his due (Matt. 22:21). Although
the immediate context was taxation rather than armaments,
it might not be a misapplication of the text to use it in support of the draft. Jesus seemed to insinuate that wars were
inevitable. Then, too, in Matthew 10:34, Jesus says that
he has not "come to send peace on the earth but a sword."

These latter statements of Jesus could be used in an
attempt to classify him as a militarist. But, we must remember that the passage on "rendering unto Caesar" was not
made in reference to supporting the draft, but in response
to a tax issue. Further, when Jesus said that there would
(always) be wars, he was not necessarily advocating them.
The Matthew 10:34 passage was not for the purpose of
teaching Christians to be militant so much as it was a statement of the controversial nature of the Kingdom of God. So
in reality, these Scriptures cannot make of Christ a belliger-

ent Messiah. Rather, most of the New Testament presents him as a pacifist.

The early church taught that war was unchristian. The New Testament was not filled with military prohibitions, but Christ had made it clear that the Kingdom of God did not depend upon military enterprise. Roland H. Bainton thought that the antimilitary spirit of early Christendom came not from any specific New Testament teaching but from an attempt on the part of these primitive disciples to discover the mind of Christ himself.[4] Tolstoy pointed to the evident contradiction in the conjunction of faith and arms:

> You are surprised that soldiers are taught that it is right to kill people in certain cases and in war, while in the book admitted to be holy by those who so teach, there is nothing like such a permission, but, on the contrary, not only is all murder forbidden but all insulting of others is forbidden also, and we are told not to do to others what we could not wish done to us. And you ask, is not this fraud? . . . Ya, it is a fraud, committed for the sake of those accustomed to living on the sweat and blood of other men, and who have therefore perverted and still pervert Christ's teaching . . .[5]

If Bainton and Tolstoy and countless others are correct in their assessment of Christ's teaching in the New Testament, by what rationale do we justify any participation in war? Emerson taught that when man had sufficiently matured, he would outgrow war-making, which was the worst product of his immaturity. But since Emerson we have had Kaiser Wilhelm, Adolph Hitler, and Joseph Stalin. Any maturity and pacification of the human spirit is not at all obvious. If anything, we seem to be getting worse rather than better, and the chances that we will outgrow war seem remote.

Assuming that Emerson is wrong and we shall have to go on living with war, when and how will we justify our participation in it? To be sure, we can never accept war as an inevitability. For centuries some have argued that man has a combative nature and that he is innately a warrior; therefore, since war is natural, it will continue. Still, we Christians are involved in the revolutionary business of change. Man is naturally a sinner, but we are unwilling to accept him as such; evangelism is our attempt to save man from his state of sin. Christians have the same responsibility to stop war as they do to stop sin.

War has had an awful portent since Nagasaki. Our universal dread of nuclear war is aptly expressed by the little boy who, when asked what he wanted to be when he grew up, said, "Alive." War has become a threat of such magnitude that we cannot accept it merely because it seems a natural part of the human spirit. Nuclear fire-storming is a grave horror whose statistical dimensions preclude its being suggested by any sane person as a meaningful solution to any political confrontation. Loudly it must be declared that war has become such an ominously destructive and threatening thing that we cannot sanction a tolerance of it. Every Christian should extend himself as far as possible in the attempt to abolish it.

Some wars, however, may be just wars that should be waged. The concept unfortunately has been open to wide rationalizations. Nearly every war is just, depending upon whom you ask—the aggressor or the defender; the victor or the vanquished. Aristotle thought that wars against barbarians were just. The Crusades were considered just because they were aimed at liberating Christian lands from heathenism. John Calvin thought there were five acceptable bases for just wars: to inflict general vengeance by a king, to preserve the peace, to contain those who sought to disturb the peace, to rescue the oppressed, and to punish crimes.[6] Still, in plain truth, the concept has been used by the worst aggressors and tyrants to render their campaigns acceptable.

In our own day the Vietnam conflict has pointed up the fact that it is often impossible to tell which wars are just and which are not. The terrorism of the Viet Cong needs to be suppressed and ended if any aura of normalcy is to return to that country. It would seem to many of us that the war there is a just war for the Americans to conduct. Still, there are sincere Communists who believe that our involvement is a threat to the independence of Southeast Asia. They believe further that a victory for the United States there would bring new economic advantages for meddlesome capitalists and would hamper the self-sufficiency of the occupied country. Thus they feel justified even in their bloody offensive and terrorism, believing that it is less an evil than an American victory.

In spite of the fact that it is difficult to determine, I still believe that there are just wars. Perhaps the key for determining which wars are just and which are not is solely a humanitarian principle. A war which is waged for the acquisition of power, land, or prestige can hardly be called a just war.

If war is ever contained or negated there must accompany the new age a spirit of international respect not hitherto managed. We must, for instance, wish for our foes liberty and the pursuit of happiness, no matter how immensely different our ideologies may be. Needless to say, this must work in both directions: our enemies also must be willing to live and let live.

We in the West will have to acquire a world loyalty that is based neither on intense national pride nor in the Christian faith. We will have to love and esteem Buddhist and Moslem nations and desire for them the highest levels of living and hope because they are men and not because they are either Democrats or Christians. We will have to have the kind of love that Joseph Fletcher has defined for the world in his studies in ethics: *agape*—love that does not necessarily embrace what a man is, but wishes for him the highest levels of dignity and happiness. World peace then might follow, but never unless, in their socio-religious culture, sister nations reciprocate with the same extension of good will. It appears so far that the Communist nations are unwilling to allow republican nations this right to exist with their systems. Until they abandon their present ideas of infiltration and conquest, therefore, coexistence cannot be a reality. Republican governments must defend themselves in just wars for the preservation of their cherished liberties.

A world loyalty which operates independently of Christianity and nationalism will be very hard for many of us to manage. Particularly will this be so for evangelical Christians. I confess readily that it will be for me. Like most Baptists, I grew up in a church which displayed on the chancel the American and Christian flags and taught an intense loyalty to both. I do not feel that this was wrong. Still, I am very much afraid that I have often been guilty of seeing them as one, and of viewing God's purpose in his world as identical with American political philosophies. With a little mature thinking, I realize now the fallacy of this rationale. Continuing to love my country intensely, I realize that she has often been wrong. As some wag pointed out, to say, "My country, right or wrong," is like saying, "My mother, drunk or sober." Further, I realize that much of her way of life and her political action does not coincide with Christian faith and in many cases has been diametrically opposite God's plan for his world.

In the case of America's war policy, we must be careful that we do not envision ourselves as carrying out the will of God by virtue of our political citizenship. We must not assume that the sword of America is the sword of Jesus. We must be careful when we mobilize the infantry that we do not look for some religious champion to sprinkle holy water on our cause, of getting the bishops to bless the armaments. Pierre Berton, in a critical look at our behavior during World War I, said:

> For on all sides of the bitterest and most useless of modern conflicts, the church was in the lead, blessing weapons, waving national banners and announcing that God was on our side . . . We have the Reverend James Denney, D.D., writing that "we are fighting for the battle of truth and humanity, which is the Lord's battle and for that reason can count on His support." [7]

On the other hand, Kaiser Wilhelm saw himself as the hands of God, and his chief general made all of his plans in collaboration with God. And in the days which preceded World War II, Pastor Albert prayed:

> Our praise is due to the first master builder, Adolf Hitler. The work that lies before us is so great that we might tremble before it unless we knew that over all stands the Lord, who gives strength and comfort, to all who call on Him. Lord, bless the work, bless the master builder . . .[8]

Such examples of "Christian Germany" equating God with the national cause make it immediately obvious that we cannot presume that any nation's campaign and the Kingdom of God are synonymous. We are in the world as God's fifth column. As Paul said, we are his ambassadors. We must, therefore, be able to see his total purpose in his global program and set this above our immediate and national loyalties.

Nationalizing God and putting him in charge of victory as a tribal icon may be in part responsible for some of the skeptics' views about God, namely, that he has caused more wars and has been used as a defense for more causes than any other pretext. Kenneth Scott Latourette once admitted that although Jesus and war were not compatible "the latter has often made it possible for the former to survive."[9]

We must let it be known that Christ is not the troublemaker he is often made out to be. He is rather the Prince of Peace. He never champions aggrandizement or war. Those in responsible authority who bear the name of Christ and call him Savior must be ready with maturity to suggest the conference table as an alternate for mature nations. President Kennedy said we must never "negotiate out of fear or fear to negotiate." But the issue for the peacemakers, whom the beatitudes call "the children of God," is not fear; it is love. War can never be harmonized with the expression of God's world-love in John 3:16. God is in love with all of his world and our enemies are not his enemies.

When war seems imminent between Christian powers, as has been true in the last two world wars, we must not quickly call God our champion and ask him to fight for us and our cause. Instead, like Telemachus of old, let us say, as we gesture toward the conference table, "In the name of Jesus Christ, forbear!"

Probably we cannot induce men to beat their armaments into plowshears and pruning hooks, but out of love we must work and dream of such an end. In accord with Jesus' own prediction we must realize that "wars and rumors of wars" may always exist. And though we may not see the end of war until that final struggle between Michael and the Dragon is all over, we are in the meantime under divine command and thoroughly owned by the Savior.

Recurrent wars may end history with holocaust. It seems less likely that Teilhard de Chardin is right when he says that the end of the world is not catastrophe but glory.[10] Still, we are not to become "peaceniks" staging a mindless happening, a protest void of suggestions, or riots without counsel. Stomping around missile sites without socks is not the route of God's peacemakers. We are to be exactly what we are—Christians speaking out, and saying something when we do!

But what can we say? How is it possible for individual Christians to have an effect on the international debates that preface war? It is difficult to answer these questions.

Though conscientious objection and antiwar protests may be helpful in some cases, they are generally unrealistic and simplistic solutions. On the other hand, the electoral power of the voter is always an opportunity to place in office level-headed and dispassionate leaders who can "keep their cool" in tense international situations. Or perhaps Christians might make known their feelings for peace through congressional lobbyists. Rapport with politicians would be the healthiest and most substantial sort of influence. Only extremists have really tried it so far; Christians might well test the effectiveness of this exercise of their antiwar conscience.

Probably the most important antiwar weaponry that Christians can have is their attitude of world concern. If Christians feel responsible for all human life, they will not be hasty either to initiate devastation or even to retaliate. The dignity which belongs to every human being regardless of his citizenship ought to dictate that we must use war only as a defensive or self-preserving measure. Even then it must come only as the final resort, when every other attempt to negotiate a settlement has failed.

One thing is sure. If we constantly talk only of spiritual reconciliation, we cannot stop war. But if it should ever become obvious that the Prince of Reconciliation is alive among the nations, they might yet lay down their arms. Perhaps then they will stretch their hands in friendship to those on the other side of the battlefields. For the world's sake, indeed for its continuance, let us publish peace.

3 Of Monks and Ministers

The ministry is for all who are called to share in Christ's life.

Elton Trueblood
The Incendiary Fellowship

THE RAILS were in the valley where it was night, but the morning sun was tipping the purple mountains with light. The Appenines at daybreak! When I had pushed my face closer to the glass of the railway coach window, I studied an Italy caught between night and day. On one particular mountaintop there was a monastery, a beautiful and strangely golden bastion in the new morning. Contrasting sharply with the vineyards and villages, still wrapped in mist and velvet in the valley below, it presided over them with a kind of smug self-righteousness.

Perhaps the tableau riveted itself in my mind because in a spiritual sense it reflected my view of monasteries. Monasteries are nearly always on the mountaintops, nearly always in the sunlight, and nearly always a safe distance from the darkened world where the "non-monks" live. Being a "non-monk" myself, I sympathize with "non-monks," and I resent the brown-robed friars for their years of spiritual indulgence and noninvolvement with the "non-monks."

Not that what they are doing is bad. On the contrary, to

pray, to chant the liturgy, to read the Holy Scriptures, to meditate upon eternity—all are gratifying and fulfilling activities. Monks have time to be good men, but their goodness is often sterile and free of germs. It has a mystical quality that most of us will never observe except through double glass, for we cannot touch it, and it will not come down from its mountaintop transcendence to touch us.

The monastery has traditionally been a place of withdrawal and spiritual safety. It is disconcerting to realize that many "non-monks" feel that same way about the church. Earl Brill commented, "All right, so I like it here in the bosom of the Holy Mother Church, where it's warm and cozy. But I've been out in that secular world and believe me it's cold outside!"[1] Who can deny it? The church is deliciously comfy! It is a refuge for the chilled spirit; it warms men's souls like a shag rug and a December fire. It is our retreat from the cold winter of political discontent, the ugly generation gap, and the engulfing despair that congeals our optimism.

There can be little doubt that the comfort of the cloister has negated, for some at least, the real idealism of the church. God never intended the church to be a stopover in the arctic of human affairs. He did not bring it into being to pull his people out of a frigid system, but rather to launch them into it. In the Bethlehem event, he was teaching us not to evade the world, but to get into it. Christians cannot hope to be like Christ if they seek to avoid what was his sole destination—the world.

This is not to say that the Christian should never look for moments to be apart from the world with his God. Certainly the ministry of Christ is replete with occasions when he isolated himself from all his associates for times of worship and communion.

But there was nothing recluse about the God-man, Jesus Christ. He lived with the ordinary people who busied themselves with common things. Like all of his friends, he never met a Caesar or wore the broad border of esteem. Like them too, he ate barley meal and seafood. He got involved in his world for its own sake, although he might have preferred to say, "Father, this place is in a mess; I will withdraw and give my life in prayer for it!"

Sadhu Sundar Singh, when he was in England, wrote back to some friends in India: "Pray for me because I am desperately tempted. I would rather spend all my time in prayer than go out and fulfill my engagements."[2] Jesus may have suffered just such temptations as this, but he never yielded. Instead, he said with the energy of conviction, "As the Father hath sent me, even so send I you." He had come to do God's redemptive work in the world, and he commissioned his disciples to do that work in that same world.

Why then do we so much enjoy withdrawing from the world? Is it because it is dangerous? Like a president without his secret protectors we are always exposed and always vulnerable. Nevertheless, there is no other way to be Jesus' disciple than to minister.

It must annoy him that many who find discipleship a burden have taken the easier route of churchmanship. Churchmanship and discipleship are not synonyms. Churchmanship is not practiced in the world nor done in the arena. It majors on secondary things, for whatever is not done as a ministry to the world is a secondary issue. Polishing candlesticks in the house of the Lord is not cross-bearing.

The Christ on the church altar is not the one who breaks the bread in the city's welfare system, or loves the orphans, or walks to Alcoholics Anonymous in search of a soul. He is immaculate in the church; he is even warm, but he is mindless and without compassion. At best, he is only Christ for his hymn-and-prayer friends. He is the out-of-the-world Christ for the out-of-the-world crowd.

Most of those to whom the church is a retreat do not practice lifelong, perpetual monasticism but have secular involvements and occupations which force them out of the church. They do not minister in his name outside, however. These incognito Christians justify their chronic withdrawal by saying that the ministers of religion are the specialists who are supposed to be the world-involved disciples.

This was exactly the problem of the monasteries during the Middle Ages, when many thought that living faith was the responsibility of the religious specialists. Dietrich Bonhoeffer wrote:

> Monasticism was represented as an individual achievement which the mass of the laity could not be expected to emulate. By thus limiting the application of the commandments of Jesus to a restricted group of specialists, the church evolved the conception of the double standard—a maximum and a minimum standard of Christian Obedience.[3]

God has made it clear that he has no such standards. He expects us to serve right where he saves us—here, in this world, at this time. We may not pretend to be interested in God, accept his salvation, and then walk off and leave his world. According to D. T. Niles, "If we want to speak with God, we had better find out something about the world because that is the only subject in which God is interested."[4] Harvey Cox said that the section of *Time* magazine which God reads last every week is Religion, and the part that he reads first is People, because God is interested in people.[5] Probably Cox is right. And it just may be that men are much more interested in religion than God is.

God's love affair with the world is an expensive one which cost him the life of his Only-begotten. It goes on costing the disciple, who must make the world aware, person by person, of God's love for men, even when men usually turn aside his love. We must not shut ourselves in our church houses and sing and preach and pretend that this is Christianity's total being. If we do not love the world much closer at hand than that they will guess that we do not love them at all.

We must demonstrate our world-love: we must practice the priesthood of the believer, seeing ourselves not only as lovers of God, but as priests of God. A priest is a "go-between," not between God and his altar, but between God and his world. Paul rather made the point when he encouraged us to be "ambassadors for Christ" (2 Cor. 5:20). We are from his embassy on a diplomatic mission to his world. His is not a second-rate power; he once testified, "All power is given unto me." It must be said, too, that his mission is strategic; without it the world will perish. It is imperative that we be priests.

The Latin word for priest—*pontifex*—means "bridge builder."

Jesus' "Go ye" is our command to build bridges wherever we can to help span the gulf between man and God. This is the only route of redemption, and it is urgent, so urgent that it must be reemphasized: *Bridge building is the ministry of Christianity.*

It is this issue of bridge building that divides the monks and the ministers. The monks know very little about it. They spend their years strengthening their own relationship, reinforcing their route to God. Gloriously the monks make secure their relationship to God, but they never help anyone else get there.

The Roman Catholics call the pope the *Pontiff*, which is short for *Pontifex maximus*, the great bridge builder. The tragedy in the modern evangelical camp is that there are few great bridge builders. Most disciples are not even *pontifeces minimi*, little bridge builders. In my own denomination, which is famous for its conservative interpretation of Scripture, it takes thirty years for the average disciple to win one other person to faith in Christ. Of course, we cannot win his beloved world with such a scanty supply of bridges. At that rate, before we get there, most people will die and go to hell looking for a way across the chasm that has always separated their lives from meaning.

The average church member never sees himself as a soulwinner. I have often been asked by my members, "Pastor, would you go see John Doe? He needs Christ in his messed-up life." What they are really saying is, "You're the specialist. It's your job to win men to Christ. It just is not my field!" They are the monks who see me as the minister.

The church is not a sweet shrine. If we do not leave church bent on winning someone to faith in Christ, we have not been to church. It is not an escape for keyed-up executives. It is the drafting room where we design the spans and calculate the stress factors so that we can then send out the ministers who will build adequately the approaches to life.

Ministering salvation is a difficult business. How to help someone know Christ requires all sorts of discipline. A minister who is famous for his witnessing and winning of men admits that he is often at a loss for wisdom and courage. On a recent flight, he was seated next to a rather large man with a self-confident air about him. In the course of conversation, he was reminded by the Holy Spirit that the man, whoever he was or however self-important he looked, might be one of the millions in search of Christ. So with firmness of resolve the minister decided to ask the man if he were a Christian. He got a part of it out before he was stopped short: "Sir," he began, "are you a———" The man in the next seat blustered an interruption: "Am I a what?" Lamely the minister said, "Are you a Northerner or a Southerner?"

All of the foibles and failures of bridge-building discourage me. It is because I believe it is so important that I do it at all, for seldom am I at ease with it. Sometimes I do not put the pier deep enough with the result that the whole structure collapses and the project fails to connect the individual to Christ. Other times I do not pave the approaches with finesse, and nothing comes of the attempt.

One thing keeps me trying: I know that there is no other way to God than Christ Jesus. Also, I know that if someone like me does not tell a person about Christ, he may never know. The Bible has taught me further that I must not presume that someone else will go about with the witness if I do not. The situation is too final for such presumption. I am responsible for his world-love and his personal redemption.

Elton Trueblood, in his *Company of the Committed*, likens the witness to a situation in the courts. The witness holds in his experience a bit of evidence that, shared with the jurors, will set the condemned man free. The witness may withold the evidence if he wishes, but if he does he will be guilty of the sentence. He may not remain silent under subpoena or he will perjure himself and suffer complete loss of integrity. In the same way, a person who witnesses to his faith must tell what he has seen and knows to be true about Christ and his Father.

Ezekiel the prophet described the responsibility of God's ambassador in a striking anecdote. God's messenger, he said, was like a watchman on the city wall. If he did not see the enemy approach the city, or if he failed to sound the trumpet and the city fell to the enemy, the entire responsibility of the ruin would be his. In the same way, the minister must witness or the loss of the unredeemed will be cause for his censure.

Winslow Homer has long been one of my favorite artists. His canvases are rugged with jagged tides, raw winds, and weathered seamen. One of my favorites pictures two sailors in rain slicks crossing over the seething sea on a cable stretched between two ships. The artist has captured their desperation; in the swelling of wind and water the cable is the only way across.

The Bible has made it clear that Christ Jesus is the only bridge across existence. "I am the way, the truth, and the life," said Jesus, "and no man cometh unto the Father but by me" (John 14:6).

We have forgotten just how desperate men are without Christ. Our forebears understood it much better than do we. They gathered in their dingy old "meetin' houses" and sang by lantern light:

> Throw out the Life Line across the dark wave,
> There is a brother whom someone should save;
> Somebody's brother, Oh, who then, will dare,
> To throw out the Life Line, his peril to share!

But we do not see the peril. We would not dream that the nicely dressed people who come into our churches so utterly at ease need to be "saved" from anything. And when, even without Christ, they lustily join in as we sing "We're Marching to Zion," we smile at them and assume that they *are* marching to Zion.

Those who served in Christ before our generation never assumed as much as do we. They knew that unless people accepted Christ as the only way to God they could never be saved. True, they had drab buildings and poor facilities, but that didn't matter; it was the bridges between God and men that were important. Now it is the buildings which are all-important and the bridges which are irrelevant.

Ministers of stature who are not religious professionals but who have given their lives to the ministry of bridges do occasionally appear. A striking example is a woman of my acquaintance whose love for Christ kept her at his commission until she was prematurely stricken with disease. The last time I saw her, she was frail and wasted beyond description. Trying to disguise my stunned reaction to seeing her so sick, I asked her how she was feeling. "Fine," she sang out, "well, almost fine. Anyway, I taught Sunday school last Sunday." It was impossible for me not to be surprised, for she could barely stand (she passed away soon after our conversation). "You taught Sunday school! You can't feel that well!" I exclaimed, with complete loss of tact. "I had to," was her matter-of-fact reply. "The regular teacher couldn't come; she had a cold." Somehow I managed to fight the stinging at the corner of my eyes, but instantly I was angry at the indifference of the teacher who had shrugged off her responsibility. She had seen it as just a class of young children, but my friend had seen it as a collection of beings who needed a bridge to the Father which she could supply. It did not matter to her that she was near the end of her own life; she was still busy building bridges for others.

A glimpse at the ministry of Jesus will reveal that he spent all of his time linking people to God. At the village well he met the divorcée from Sychar; in the midnight shadows he reasoned with Nicodemus; in the press of his popularity he beckoned to Zacchaeus in the tree; at the customhouse he nodded to Matthew; in the cemetery, he

confronted the insane Legion; on the tree he whispered to
the criminal about paradise and life—literally everywhere
he went he built the bridges that men might know life
eternal.

Now he is away and the task is ours. We must love his
beloved and speak to them of him. We must tell them that
all of God is theirs for calling Christ Lord. We must
minister.

Paul Scott by his own admission was once a man in search
of a bridge. Crippled by leprosy while in adolescence, he
finally reached a stalemate with the disease. Partially blinded
and severely eroded physically, for a while he felt as though
there was nothing to live for. Then through an unusual chain
of circumstances he managed to get an appointment with
Bishop Fulton Sheen. When he saw the bishop he said, "I've
come to you because I have no one else to turn to; I haven't
a friend in the world." "Well, now you have," the bishop
smiled. Their friendship grew over successive weeks, as
they lunched and visited together. Lots of good things came
from their relationship, but most of all was the new access
which Paul began to discover toward God: "Faith and belief are with me all the time and I don't have to consciously
dwell on it. They are there—just as God is—and I can live
in that assurance day by day." [6]

Fulton Sheen, like every great man of God, has been a
builder of bridges, exposing God's love for men and inviting
them to Christ. But there are not enough preachers and
bishops to handle all the needs of the unsaved world. If we
are ever to make a dent in the universal need, every man
who names Christ his Lord must take up the rescue work.
The planet will go unredeeemed if we depend upon the
sermons and the liturgies to do the whole job.

God, who knows how well we worship, must discover how
well we can work. And when we minister, we shall hear
some person who has looked for life and meaning say, "Today I found God and life is new!"

4 *The Huksters*

A house built on sand will not last; neither will a civilization built on dirt.

Norman Vincent Peale
Sin, Sex, and Self-Control

A HUCKSTER is "one who peddles small wares." Such peddlers must do all they can to make their wares appear both desirable and necessary. Making them gaudy with spangles and glitter, they conceal the truth that underneath the sequins is the poorest grade of chalk and plaster.

Hucksters in yesteryear came in a predictable assortment of vaudeville stripes and straw hats, and they "barked" their suitcase items in a carnival-midway nasality. Some of them these days are peddling laissez-faire sex, and today's thrill-seeking and bored populace seems to like the glittering, second-rate morality. Though individuals are still punished by law for exhibitionism, society as a whole seems to thrive on immoral exposure.

Playwrights, novelists, entertainers, movie producers, and even theologians are involved in the big sex-sell. The fact that their backgrounds are varied has in no way diminished their expanding volume of bargain-counter sexuality. It is very clearly a hard sell. Sometimes they peddle their wares in

velvet and fishnet and candlelight. The ad men sell it along
with liquor, cigarettes, automobiles, and mouthwash. The
cultured sell it under the name of "art"; the intellectual, under the name of "realism." It has been given official license
by the New Moralists, who grant indulgence unconditionally
if one's motives are sufficiently "other-centered."

The hucksters are too numerous for listing. Often they are
prestigious people who could actually make worthy contri-
butions to the wealth of culture and wisdom stockpiled by
human genius in every corner of history but who seem content to peddle their dubious chalk and spangles in lieu of
greater items. Though in their labors there are some virtues
and honor, they have succeeded in killing the aura of dignity
which sexual expression ought to own. By undressing it in
the marketplace, they have made it grotesque and absurd.

The peddlers have seen their books and movies soar in
sales. Their plays, magazines, mail-order pornography, party
records, and the other assorted forms of marketable indecen-
cies abound. The sheer volume of their smut-production has
inevitably played a part in shaping new sexual attitudes. The
hucksters have unwittingly or otherwise been responsible
for the cultic reverence now lavished on sex and the ensuing
wave of libertinism which has issued from it.

In this new wave of liberality, the difference between sex
and filth has become blurred. A spade of ground in the
garden is soil, but on the carpet in the parlor it is just plain
dirt. Similarly, sex, when considered within the framework
of marriage and Christian perspective, is beautiful and possessed of dignity, but in the novel and the cinema it has
become filth more often than not.

Sex must be recognized as a legitimate and necessary
human drive. It is God's gift to be used and enjoyed. But it is
also to be respected and controlled. Hunger is a basic human
drive, too; without our appetite for food, we might be indif-
ferent to our physical well-being. But it is obvious that over-
indulgence in food can destroy and lead to death prematurely.
The person who gluttonously sates his appetite for food is

discarding his self-respect and well-being. Perhaps it needs to be said that we have now come to the place where we are practicing sexual gluttony.

We have lost our self-control. Will Durant said it very well:

> Sex, after hunger, is our strongest instinct and greatest problem. Nature is infatuated with continuance, and dolls up the woman with beauty and the man with money to lure them into continuing the species; and so it gives to us males such sensitivity to the charms of women that we can go quite mad in their pursuit. Sex then becomes a fire and a flame in the blood, and burns up the whole personality— which should be a hierarchy and harmony of desires.
>
> Our ancestors played this sexual impulse down, knowing that it was strong enough without encouragement; we have blown it up with a thousand forms, of incitation, advertisement, emphasis and display, and have armed it with the doctrine that inhibition is dangerous. Whereas inhibition— the control of impulse—is the first principle of civilization.[1]

This *control of impulse* is doubly hard to manage because the hucksters are always blasting away at our inhibitions. They have devised a new list of "profane words" which nearly everyone tries to avoid: prudish, Victorian, puritan, naïve, out-of-it. To many, these labels mark the end of their cosmopolitan, mature self-image, so they traffic in the new, omni-available sex.

The result has been that those who defend a more traditional morality have found themselves on the outside of contemporary literature and entertainment. "Adults only" does not usually mean that no minors or adolescents are admitted; it simply means "adult fares only." But the phrase does indicate a kind of reading or entertainment which is morally questionable and completely unacceptable to those who practice Christian decency. A movie suitable for the average family is nearly a "Disney-only" consideration. The popularity of the few such movies which are produced is evidence that the hucksters have not been entirely successful.

There are still a host of men and women who are not buying. It may be that they have realized that the sex salesmen spell the name of their product $ex. The dollar sign seems the symbol of their trade just as the caduceus is the escutcheon of modern medicine. They are in the business clearly for the money, and they know that smut sells and sells quickly. At the zenith of its popularity *Valley of the Dolls* was selling 100,000 paperbacks every 24 hours. Bunny Clubs across the nation are dispensing sophisticated sex for soaring profits. In a frantic competition for viewing markets television and movies are like two school boys seeing who can get the most attention with vulgarisms. Max Rafferty says that in Los Angeles alone, 700,000 copies of "girlie" magazines are printed every month and that California's eight major publishers turn out 1,500,000 dirty paperbacks every thirty days. He further said that obscene photos and films bring a million dollars in profits to that state every year.

It may be that non-buyers have further realized that there is no social edification in the sex swindle. Decades ago the hucksters were saying that when they had dragged sex out of its Victorian shell and exposed it in the sun of education and science and secularism, the world would be free from the curse of bad conditioning, and we would be emancipated from bootleg immorality. But the cultural aspects of their revolution never happened along. Divorce increased, and so did illegitimacy. Venereal disease exploded. The anti-puritans failed in their promise of enlightenment and health and stable home life.

It may be that those who have not haggled with the hucksters are aware that they are in business solely for themselves, thinking neither of the commonwealth or individual home life. Individual good is unimportant, so long as their system prospers. They traffic in illegitimacy and broken lives. Their awareness of the national milieu does not slack their promotion or production. The presses must roll their pornography, both the semi-decent and legal, and the indecent and illegal. The celluloid film must travel through the projectors in America's theaters. The hucksters are for the hucksters, in business for themselves.

In contrast to this concept is the Christian view; not just of sex, but all of life. Christians are under command to be others-centered. In fact, Dietrich Bonhoeffer called Jesus the Man for others. All that He did was for others: healing, teaching, saving others—these things were Jesus' life. The Christian is never free to ask "What can this person or this experience mean to me?" or "How may I exploit this person or this part of my world?" Our commission is to be for others and not to see what we can get from them.

How then may the Christian confront the peddlers of the new sex? No one likes hypocritical people or philosophies, and the temptation is to praise the new men who destroyed the hypocrisy of the Victorian Era. In a way it seems that the hucksters have saved us from the black-market immorality that existed in the baroque closets of days now gone. But though the idea seems right, we must remember that some things which are wrong are very close to being right.

Running through the Rocky Mountains, the granite spine of our nation, is the Great Divide; water which falls west of that line ends up in the Pacific Ocean, and water which falls east of the divide flows to the Atlantic. Theoretically, two drops of water falling one inch apart on either side of that line could wind up in immensely different places. Similarly, the facts which are given to us by the sex revolutionaries may appear right, but wind up in immensely different places. Are the hucksters our salvation from bad science, or our damnation?

Perhaps we need to look at sexual freedom in the realm of interpersonal relations. When we are suddenly coerced by the law at the point where our freedoms must end, we will often insist that the law be bent, our misdemeanor excused, our freedom extended to a traffic speed five miles per hour greater than everyone else's, and that charges be dropped. We desire freedom in sex too (let us not forget that the sex drive

is just one of our God-created drives), but we must realize
that with every sort of freedom there comes corresponding
responsibility.

So then, the ultimate question probably is this: How do
we keep in balance two very important freedoms, the freedom to fill our appetites and the freedom from gray and
nagging guilt? To some of the hucksters the answer is simply
to shuck conscience, and from then on the freedom for any
sort of indulgence will be automatic and fun. Probably this
is Helen Gurley Brown's kind of rationale when she insists
that sex is fun, so why not enjoy it? This freedom without
guilt may have been in Hemingway's mind when he wrote:
"What is good is what you feel good after, what is immoral
is what you feel bad after." [2] This latitude is a bit too wide
for an irresponsible conscience.

Joseph Fletcher feels that one may be comfortable with
broad license, so long as his every indulgence is motivated
by *agape*—love for the other person or persons involved. If
an act is committed with the other person's welfare as the
greater motivation, then it is good and right. His school assumes (falsely, I believe) that the rational dedication to serve
others' ends are more powerful than the biological and
egotistical cravings to serve our own.

Sexual freedom is encouraged by the concept that interpersonal sex is a private affair and that what is done in
private between consenting parties is hardly immoral. Dr.
Fletcher said in his *Situation Ethics* that anything done in
love (using his definition) and in private so that it does not
"frighten the horses" is moral. But in his *Moral Responsibility*, he recognizes that people are generally prone to grant
themselves sexual permission for widely different reasons,
most of which never get near his concept of *agape*. He
frankly admits girls often play at sex in search of love, while
young men often play at love in search of sex. This kind of
sexual motivation is inadequate and this kind of freedom is
immoral.

Jesus considered even permissive thinking mental indulgence and therefore wrong: "Ye have heard that it was said by them of old time, Thou shalt not commit adultery; But I say unto you that whosoever looketh on a woman to lust after her hath committed adultery with her already in his heart" (Matt. 5:27–28).

If the Master outlawed mental license, then surely the Christian moral standard sees any kind of permissiveness as sin. It is clear from the Bible that interpersonal sexual freedom outside of marriage is neither a personal improvement nor a cultural improvement.

Besides, the freedom is clearly illusory. Sexual permissiveness is not really freedom, for those who practice it are in bondage to a guilt and sin that is more than just the result of Victorian brainwashing. There is the feeling that God is displeased by the transgression of the Seventh Commandment.

The freedom is illusory because often the unmarried couple who participate are at every moment afraid of discovery and embarrassment. One father illustrated this when he reminded his daughter of the fear involved in illicit sex. She was willing to wait, but she found it difficult to understand why in a world where freedom seemed in vogue. Her father reminded her that the real freedom she was seeking could come only within the context of marriage:

> I think I can tell you in six words what you are waiting for. You are waiting to be free. Free from the nagging voice of conscience and the gray shadow of guilt. Free to give all of yourself, not a panicky fraction.[3]

Any other idea of real sexual freedom is unworthy.

Whatever the hucksters say, premarital or extramarital permissiveness is not a form of freedom, but bondage. It is a bondage which not only affects all of one's affairs before marriage, but casts the pall of guilt over marriage itself. Pearl Buck's novel *The New Year* is a tale of the consequences of extramarital permissiveness, where the child of an illicit affair later comes like a specter into a happy home

and unfolding career and threatens both. Certainly this is
not freedom.

Psychiatrists who have probed the ugly marital tangles
of our day find at the root of many such problems a gnawing
guilt for some sexual liberty that may have occurred years
before. "Liberty" is obviously a misnomer. Shakespeare put
it well when he had Prospero say to Ferdinand:

> If thou dost break her virgin knot before
> All sanctimonious ceremonies may
> With full and holy rite be ministered,
> No sweet aspersion shall the heavens let fall
> To make this contract grow; but barren hate,
> Sour-eyed disdain and discord, shall bestrew
> The union of your bed with weeds so loathly
> That you shall hate it both.
> —*The Tempest*

The biblical principles of chastity and marital integrity
are the real avenues of freedom. Discipline and self-control
are surer paths to marital happiness than the permissiveness
of the peddlers. We must conclude that all of the rationalizations of these moral liberators and the actions based on them
most often have a destructive rather than an edifying effect.

The biblical concept of purity and one man for one
woman, conversely, does lead to fulfillment and the kind of
freedom which has no gray zones of regret. In this kind of
moral atmosphere the person is entirely free to develop and
enlarge his personality. The president of a fashion agency
said to one of the models who had gotten involved in a deep
love tangle:

> Nothing will break down a woman's beauty faster than a
> love affair outside her marriage, whether it is because she
> is afraid of losing her husband or because she is leading a
> guilty life. The cosmetics inventor who discovers how to
> recapture the serenity of a happily married woman will be-
> come a millionaire overnight. There is no cream or powder
> in the world that can duplicate the kind of contented color
> and light that shines in a woman who knows that she be-
> longs to one man and that man belongs to her.[4]

The new openness is not the dawn of a beautiful ideology; it is rather the crumbling of decency. It is plainly a sexual tragedy for our immediate world.

Consider its end. Between 1940 and 1957 illegitimacy increased 112 percent in the 15–19-year-old age group in our nation and 300 percent in the 20–24-year-old age group. In some American cities venereal disease has increased over 500 percent in a decade. By 1970 ten million Americans had been born out of wedlock; in simpler numbers that is nearly one out of twenty. These grim statistics go on and on ad infinitum. And the hucksters have the gall to tell us that we have been emancipated. We are clearly shackled by our libertinism.

Statistics are cold. We are bored with graphs, charts, adding machines, and research books. But hidden in the files of numbers and percentages are a host of heartaches and broken homes. Such uncommunicating statistics may really indicate the broken heart of an unwed mother or the forfeit of a potential, fine career by a young man who must marry too soon. In the columns of numbers are children who are shuttled with all of their insecurities through divorce courts like the other family possessions.

"Sexual emancipation" steals the future from the indulgent and robs thousands of young lives of their right to achieve. There is no new plateau of dignity or education or better community in the new idealism of the hucksters.

They have been wrong about other things too. There is no real connection between "love" and extramarital sex. *Playboy* magazine revealed the shortcomings in its brand of deviation with a cartoon which appeared in its pages. Pictured was a rumpled young female in the arms of a man who was saying to her, "Why speak of love at a time like this?" The hucksters are not selling love. They are selling a cheap and bawdy version of intimacy where love is not even decimally involved.

Indeed, we seem to have arrived at the day when love is a secondary consideration, sought only by naïve squares and Victorian moralists. People have lost personhood. They have

become "ids," "things," "appetite-saters." Many of our youth,
lost in the bewildering jungle of accessible sex, have stopped
looking for the proper person and gone on a hunt for "fulfilling" experiences. Sexual intercourse, which was once the
most sacred of intimacies between young lovers, is often a
fifth-hand matter; it has been exploited and lost its unique
meaning.

Other young people have indulged idealistically in premarital sex in quest of love. One young girl who went the
love-via-sex route wrote later:

> Everything you read in books about love is a bunch of lies.
> It isn't tender; it isn't sweet and it isn't enduring. It is cruel
> and it hurts. Movie writers in this country ought to be
> jailed for writing all that junk about moonlight and roses
> . . . it isn't like that at all. It hurts. . . . Moreover you
> feel terrible the next day when your boy friend won't even
> look at you.[5]

Of course, the guilt diminishes somewhat with continued
indulgences. Consciences ultimately dulled, the promiscuous
rationalize their guilt feelings so that they can carry through
with barely a blush. But even those who become that calloused still know that they are not even getting close to love in
their looseness. Whatever else the sex-peddlers are hawking,
it is not love. Their whole philosophy ends in vacant fulfillment, and a heavily masqueraded decency. In short, they are
building a world of counterfeit emotions and pathological
put-ons. They are ending love for those who follow them
through their erotic wonderland.

There is one other thing the hucksters have been wrong
about. They insinuate that sexual indulgence is evidence of
maturity and an exodus from naïveté, that those who let their
inhibitions loose are part of the new smart and worldly control group. They are proud of their kind of experiential
wisdom that comes from having "been around," and they
brag about having broken out of their confining mores and
narrow little customs.

This is the obvious philosophy behind Hefnerism. Bunny clubs peg their large memberships with the idea that they are a part of a mature group with a sophisticated understanding of sex and an executive and efficient use of it. Sex, they rationalize, is a very natural appetite, and "bunnies" are a mature man's way of dealing with this particular kind of biological need.

Is this really the case, however? Harvey Cox does not think so. It is his idea that the subscription list of *Playboy* magazine is by and large filled with immature and insecure males seeking an identity they are afraid they do not have:

> The comic book that appeals to a younger generation with an analogous problem skillfully intersperses illustrations of incredibly muscled men . . . with advertisements for body-building gimmicks . . . Thus the thin-chested comic-book readers . . . are thoughtfully supplied with both the ends and the means for attaining a spurious brand of maturity. *Playboy* merely continues the comic-book tactic for the next age group. Since within every identity crisis, whether in the teens or the twenties, there is usually a sexual identity problem, *Playboy* speaks to those who desperately want to be a man and more specifically a male in today's world.[6]

The fact that neither love nor maturity is a by-product of libertinism should be enough in itself to cause the person seriously toying with the concept to abandon it. For the Christian, there is yet a stronger reason to refuse involvement in the new sex standard. We know that for centuries the Scriptures have been the guide to Christian conduct in every realm, and its men of wisdom were explicit in their common idea of morality and godliness.

It would be a mistake to assume that the hucksters are of such recent origin and the Scriptures so ancient that the latter had nothing to say about the former. Rather, these hucksters are as ancient as the Bible itself. In Abraham's day they had turned Sodom and Gomorrah into cities of prostitution and homosexuality. In Moses' lifetime, they were making golden calves and encouraging the nation into every sort of libertinism. In the years of Amos the prophet, a father and son were frequenting the same prostitute, so widespread was the moral illness of their nation.

The Bible has not changed its text on this subject. It has said the same thing to people in every generation who are tempted by the hard-sell pressure of the hucksters. Moses said tersely, "Thou shalt not commit adultery!" Paul with his love of systematic theology said it more esoterically:

> I beseech you therefore, brethren, by the mercies of God, that ye present your bodies a living sacrifice unto God, which is your reasonable service. And be not conformed to this world, but be ye transformed by the renewing of your mind.
> —Romans 12:1–2a

The Bible teaches no other course than self-discipline to achieve this purity. We must fight temptation constantly and earnestly if we are ever to defeat it. As Jesus suggested, we must not even allow ourselves mental permission, or we "will have done the act already in our hearts." We must abstain from every appearance of evil. When Harry Emerson Fosdick was a chaplain in France, a young American officer came to him. "At home I never went to a brothel," he said. "Now, I have gone twice to look on. The first time it disgusted me, the second time I tolerated it, if I were to go the third time, I know I would participate in it. . . ."

Every man comes to a time when he would like to set his moral restraints free. But the man who can see the issue far enough in advance not to allow his weakened will to bind his decency will be a happier and better man. Common sense decrees it. The Bible has promised it for twenty centuries. Whatever the hucksters are saying, the truth remains that only those who honor their responsibilities will ever be free.

5

The
Great
Contemporary

Jesus Christ the same yesterday, today, and forever.

Hebrews 13:8

IRRELEVANCY is the newest of the clichés and ugliest of the newer accusations against the church. "Get with it," say the Christian secularists who feel that the church is quite "out of it all." To them, Christianity is as quaint and unrelated to the space age as the one-horse shay is to the interstate highway system.

The dissidents seem not to notice the rowdiness of their protest against the irrelevance of the church. Or perhaps they enjoy jangling the nervous system of those who find the vestry restful and the sanctuary a retreat from the hectic life of technopolis. Those who seek rest in the church do not like their peace disturbed. But the new militant knights feel some socio-linear urge to use their lance as a probe to goad the meditating fellowship back out into the marketplace.

The basic cause of the widely separated poles may be the difference in their visualization of Christ. The traditionalists see him as the Lord of the Twenty-third Psalm leading them from secular madness to the green pastures and the still waters of private worship. The innovators see him as the Christ of the scourge with his knotted lash flogging the money

51

changers, cleansing the decadent social structure, and driving the Christians away from their retreat and into the insane world.

But there is yet another group which see Christ forever dressed in his first-century garb, as remote as a Roman temple. Most of them would not put it this way, but the actual truth is that millions of churchgoers have no vital concept of a contemporary Christ who has and seeks the right to be involved. They cannot get him out of the stained-glass windows and into a blue worsted suit and a bowler hat. They cannot conceive of him clean-shaven, with a trim haircut, boarding a TWA 747 jet and carrying in his wallet an American Express card. Their total concept of Christ is a primary Sunday-school-card impression.

We have a great need to see the gospel in modern dress. The Great Physician must appear more like a Mayo Clinic surgeon than a prop from a nativity set. The world generally is turned off by all the "thees" and "thous" which issue in sacred oratory from the men of cloth. A hymn of my acquaintance serves to illustrate our devotion to yesteryear's terminology and theology:

> Here I raise mine Ebenezer,
> Hither by thy help I'm come,
> And I hope by thy good pleasure
> Safely to arrive at home.

I could not help wondering during the singing of this hymn recently in my church, how many there had even the foggiest of notions what an Ebenezer was. And on the very Sunday that three astronauts were hurtling around the world in an Apollo spacecraft, there we all were singing in Elizabethan English, "Come Thou Fount of Every Blessing."

Of course, there is a real and vital concept of worship in hymn singing, even in the very hymn just referred to. The trouble is simply that we have convinced ourselves that archaic English is a little more sacrosanct than modern English, and austerity seems more important than understanding. And similarly we find a reverence for Christ in his first-century trappings that we could not manage if we saw him as a real contemporary.

Perhaps it would be good for us to remember that the reason our Lord came preaching in the tunic and toga and the flowing robes of two thousand years ago is that those were the common dress of his time. He spoke his Sermon on the Mount in Aramaic, the common language of his people; it was not in some Elizabethan Aramaic full of austerity and dignity, but in the simpler speech of the fishermen and publicans who were listening to him. He belonged quite naturally to his day.

That he does not seem to belong so naturally to ours is not his fault. He is quite as much alive today as he was back then, but we have not made him appear that way.

His good news too seems a little unrelated. Everywhere one sees some sensitive person straining to make Christ and his gospel contemporary. The fact that many of these people have gone overboard in this attempt must not allow us to miss the implication of all of these "get-relevant" efforts. The need has been made obvious even if the way to do it has not.

The writing of Carl F. Burke and Clarence Jordan may illustrate how far afield some have gone with this contemporizing process. Burke's *God Is for Real, Man* is a recast of biblical passages in the language and events of the city. In this book, the parable of the Prodigal Son is called "Throwin' a Party for Junior"; the temptation experiences of Jesus, "Don't Try to Con God"; and Judas's betrayal, "A Stoolie in Jesus' Gang." In unbelievably degenerate slang, the Scriptures and their Christ appear not so much contemporary as profane.

With much better taste, Clarence Jordan did the same thing in his *Cotton Patch Version of Paul's Epistles*. In his paraphrase of 2 Corinthians, which he calls II Atlanta, he has the apostle recount the perils which he has endured. Imprisonment, shipwreck, stonings, and beatings (see 2 Corinthians 11:23ff.) are likened to the chain-gang, maulings by the state-patrol, being clubbed with night sticks, car

wrecks, being shot, and narrowly escaping the Ku Klux
Klan in Savannah. However we may feel about them, such
attempts as these to make the Scriptures more contemporary
do have something to say about the world's hunger for a
relevant word from the Lord.

Some have accused the church not only of irrelevancy but
noninvolvement too. The response to the charge of noninvolvement has been interesting, where there has been a
response. Less evangelical groups have hurried off with their
placards and petitions in the direction of social action, while
the more evangelical groups have hurried off with their
handbills and posters to promote some evangelistic crusade or
rally where some "Gospel star" will be featured as the speaker
of the evening.

Involvement is a risky business, for in it the church runs
the chance of exposure. Whether it succeeds or fails in
making the Good News relevant, there will be a photo finish
in which it is observed. Needless to say, the church is no
different from us in how it feels about that. We only enjoy
being observed if we are winning a race, but we will slink by
the winner's circle if we come in last. If the church comes out
a winner in its worldly involvement, it will be strengthened
for generations yet to come. If, however, its involvement
does not bear any significant fruit, it might embarrass, or
worse, actually eviscerate Christ's church.

The peril which the church risks in its involvement may
be causing some churchmen to retreat deeper into the security
of their cloister. In *The Fall*, Albert Camus shows two
strangers coming to a bridge in old Amsterdam late at night.
As they draw near the bridge, one of them terminates the
conversation by saying,

"I'll leave you near this bridge. I never cross a bridge at
night. It's the result of a vow. Suppose, after all, that someone should jump in the water. One of two things—either you
do likewise to fish him out and, in cold weather, you run a
great risk! Or you forsake him there and suppressed dives
sometimes leave one strangely aching. Good night." [1]

The church may have this same nuisance of a conflict in some of its segments. If these members get into the arena they will either be forced to attempt a rescue and run a risk to their own well-being, or they will ignore a needy world and suffer remorse of conscience merely for having seen it and having done nothing.

Yet the only way to make Jesus contemporary is to get him out where the risks are. The church should not be afraid that he cannot take the exposure. He lived his whole life exposed. He was forever in the open where the establishment, both religious and political, could fire away at him.

Jesus preferred to live among the risks because that is where the people lived. For instance, he was willing to risk the wrath and banishment of the Gadarean aristocracy when their swine rushed over a precipice and perished in the sea. The loss of so large a herd of pigs was certain to set these men against him, yet he seemed willing to accept the risk in order to see the madman sitting clothed and in his right mind. Only by subjecting himself to criticism and exile could Jesus make him a whole person.

The blind man healed on the Sabbath is another example. Christ knew that to violate sabbatical tradition would bring on him the scorn and repudiation of officialdom. But right in the center of all those "blue laws" lay a sightless old man whose darkness could not wait another day. Jesus, in a form of civil disobedience, willingly risked the criticism he knew would come when he restored the man's sight on the Sabbath.

The supreme example of the involved Christ is the crucifixion. He longed to save men who without him would have been lost and forever damned. His desire to save them was so great that he went up to the Passover in A.D. 27 knowing that the fires of hatred smoldered against him for his anti-traditionalism and his claim to Messiahship. He could not ignore the need of men who longed for his touch to redeem them from affliction, sin, meaninglessness, death.

Have men outgrown their need for God—the involved, incarnate God that we find in Christ? Indeed not. Like every age we are estranged from God by our poor living and our sin; we need the contemporary Christ here with us. Paul Tillich put it this way:

> Despair is "the sickness unto death." But the terrible thing about the sickness of despair is that we cannot be released, not even through open or hidden suicide. For we all know that we are bound eternally and inescapably to the Ground of our being. The abyss of separation is not always visible. But it has become more visible to our generation than to the preceding generations, because our feeling of meaninglessness, emptiness, doubt, and cynicism—all expressions of despair, of our separation from the roots and the meaning of our life. Sin in its most profound sense, sin, as despair, abounds amongst us.[2]

With Tillich we confess a need for a help outside ourselves, and we are forced to admit that without it the world can never be rescued.

Christendom of late is obsessed with self-analysis. Dialogue is often built around pessimistic introspection where several are asking the question, "Is God great enough to cope with the mess?" Christ's church, originally set in motion as a rescue team for a lost world, has taken to analyzing her rescue operations and even debating their value. Her members are content to sit in their churches and seminaries discussing the seaworthiness of the lifeboats instead of manning them.

It is a mistake to assume that the world has progressed beyond God's rescuing capability. Every generation imagines itself in worse straits than any preceding generation. John Osborne, in his famous play, has Luther say in his October 31st speech in 1517, "We are living in a dangerous time. You may not think so, but it could be that this is the most dangerous time since the light first broke upon the earth." [3] And later in the same play old Staupitz says, "I heard the other day they're saying the world's going to end in 1532." [4]

In 1656 the Fifth Monarchists, a millennial group in England, were saying that the world was hopelessly, irretrievably in chaos and that nothing would redeem it except the second coming of Christ, which would occur that very year. Mother Shipton, seeing the end of her hopeless world, enmeshed in war and taxes and blood, intoned a poetic curse:

> The world to an end shall come
> In Eighteen Hundred and Eighty-one.[5]

H. G. Wells wrote in *Mind at the End of Its Tether*, "The end of everything we call life is close at hand and cannot be evaded."

Each epoch seems to be preoccupied with the hopelessness of its destiny. But precisely the meaning of the emergence of the God-man Christ Jesus is that no man is hopeless, nor is the world. Christ is our contemporary and he can salvage the world if we make him a part of it.

The resurrection is more than the central miracle of Christianity; it is also the one act of God that has insured that Christ can never become obsolete. "He is risen" does not mean that he came alive again just for the men of that faraway day. It means that he is alive forevermore and that he is literally the living Savior for men of every generation. Paul could call him friend. Jerome could too. He was the living companion of Augustine, St. Francis, Wycliffe, Thomas More, Charles Wesley, Dwight Moody, and Billy Graham. The resurrection means that he has become the great contemporary of every generation, and that he has saved from out of history all who saw him as powerful and involved in their particular age.

We must abandon the idea that our age is different, that it has outgrown his redemption, and that finally the Lord of the empty tomb has become powerless and of no consequence. Dietrich Bonhoeffer, martyred by the Nazi party, said many things and is accused of saying many things that he probably never intended to say. I will not presume to offer an interpretation or a misinterpretation of any of his statements. One of them, however, is a haunting theme for us who serve Christ two and a half decades later:

> The thing that keeps coming back to me is, what is Chris-
> tianity, and indeed what is Christ for us to-day? . . . We
> are proceeding towards a time of no religion at all.[6]

This statement of Bonhoeffer's, and others like it, set the
theologians astir with the concept of religionless Christianity.
It may be that it will come, or perhaps it is here. One thing is
sure, however: there will never be a Christless Christianity.
He will forever live and reign and save with or without a
religious or doctrinal framework; we have the Bible promise
of that. His "Lo, I am with you always" is his promise of
relevance and saving power in every generation which has
succeeded that statement.

A student of the artist Doré once came to him with a
painting of Christ, still wet on the canvas. The student asked
for an evaluation of the work. The master was silent, but the
student pressed him. The older painter was sullen and it was
evident that he thought the painting was less than striking.
Finally, upon repeated urgings from the novice, the old
artist answered, "You don't love him or you would have
painted him better." [7]

We are scarcely painting him at all because our devotion
to him is in such sad repair. How badly the world needs a
new glimpse of him! How desperately we need someone to
tell us that Christ is our contemporary, that he specializes in
healing tangled living, forgiving our plaguing guilt, and
guaranteeing our insecure futures.

Those who never know the great Contemporary will from
time to time guess that somewhere there must lie a larger
dimension. They will feel then that man has some destiny
larger than the space race. Each of them when he is quite
alone will cry out into the silence around him for something to
give his life meaning.

Without Christ, man's lost reverence will be inverted and
turned back again upon himself. He will never be satisfied
with this odd narcissism. And in his preoccupation with himself it will be harder than ever for him to stumble upon a love
for Christ, where his love might have been directed. Roger

Mehl has said: "Our age has a concern and even an obsession with *man*." [8] Arnold Toynbee believes the same thing about man's preoccupation with himself. It is his theme that man's greatest reverence through the ages has been the worship of his own power. Toynbee admits the shortcomings in this system: first of all, man isn't God; and second, he cannot find the right attitude for his suffering. Self-reverence will prevent him from discovering the deeper meaning of the love of God.

Redemption, throughout the Scriptures, has only come to those who were willing to remember that God was their able contemporary. This is the heart of the psalmist's cry in Psalm 46:1, "God is our refuge and strength, a very present help in trouble." The present God redeemed Moses and his followers from the peril of Egypt. This contemporary Jehovah was the salvation of Shadrach, Meshach, and Abednego. The living Christ delivered Bartimaeus to light and the Samaritan woman to self-respect and decency. But in every case, redemption came, and comes, to those whose understanding of God is sufficiently contemporary to allow them to call on him in their need.

Perhaps the acute spiritual needs of our world exist largely because there has been no real cry for deliverance. And there has been none because there has been no real comprehension of the contemporary Christ. Churchgoers have seen him too often in Flemish art to see him on the subway. Nor can they imagine him in line at the courthouse to pay his taxes, or at the car wash, or at the laundromat. In the very places where they spend their lives they have never encountered him. He simply does not belong to their world.

Perhaps it seems vulgar to say that Christ belongs in such ordinary places as the depots, the cafeterias, and the supermarkets. If so, we need to remember what we have already examined—the Incarnation, the God-man, the Christ on earth. This was the Bethlehem spectacular—God with us! He lived in the dust, perspired in his shop, shoved his muscled arm into his adze, and gritted his teeth over the piles of new shavings that fell to the floor. He drank from the same jar as James and Jude and his sisters. He worshiped at the synagogue in the tradition of his people. He went about in the most ordinary way doing the most ordinary things, simply living like everybody else. Jesus lived as a contemporary in his world, and he is our contemporary too.

The only way he can be our contemporary is for us to "practice his presence." We can "contemporize" Christ by using a built-in system of memoranda: First we must call to conscious awareness the thought that he really is alive and is here beside us right now. By maintaining constant awareness of his reality in the world, we will begin to change and act as though we were in the very presence of the Christ we are mentally affirming.

Perhaps the reader will feel that this is little more than auto-suggestion—a kind of selling-yourself-a-bill-of-goods. Realistically, however, it is not this at all. We do not have to create a living Christ. Rather, this contemporizing begins with the assumption that Christ already is alive, but forgotten in the current social preoccupations. St. Paul once said "Pray without ceasing." Perhaps he was in reality saying, "Contemporize! Think Christ into the current world."

If this "Christ-think" seems simplistic and inadequate, realize this: he will only live in the world to the degree that we allow him to live in our awareness. If we shut him out of mind, we shut him out of our world. He will not live in a world whose consciousness does not include him.

For the risen Christ to be a reality actually indwelling the throngs of people who have been talking about him all along, "Christ-think" is imperative. The practice would enable us to see him as certainly as did the men who walked with him long ago. It would free him from the Elizabethan gospels and make of him a current, forceful Contemporary. The benediction of the new age may yet become "Jesus Christ, the same yesterday, today, and forever."

6 *The Proper Cause*

Cassandra, the world's on fire . . .

Horace Gregory
Years of Protest

SPARTACUS, Washington, Bonaparte, Lenin, Che Guevara, Stokely Carmichael—all were rebels. Their contemporaries could not think in moderation about them; they either hated them passionately or revered them. While in the West it might seem treasonous to mention General Washington and Che Guevara in the same phrase, we must realize that our distaste for the Cuban terrorist in the 1960s could scarcely be greater than was the British distaste for General Washington in the 1770s. Lenin's praise in one section of our world is as great as disdain for him in another. Carmichael is loved as intently by the few as he is loathed by the many. The defiant ones cannot have the luxury of moderate friends. All emotions are extreme; all dialogue is critically intense.

Today's rebellion is no different. Feelings for and against it run high. The modern establishment sees our defiant youth as troublemakers whose only purpose is to keep the world in a stew. They have terribly misunderstood that the new rebellion is fired by idealism, not hooliganism. The rebels are earnestly trying to make the world a better place; and, while it may often be true that they are going about it incorrectly, it must nevertheless be admitted that they are acting when most of the world has simply ignored its problems.

I like idealism and its champions although I do not always agree with their methods. It is right that students be concerned about poverty and racism; when enough people join in that concern, perhaps we can eliminate both those ills. But nothing bothers me quite so much as to see a champion with a second-rate banner or a rebel with a third-rate cause.

Most of us are interested in a number of causes. For instance, all of us would like to see the permanent abolition of war, nonproliferation of nuclear weapons, the easing of world famine, and the end of prejudice and discrimination. All these causes must have our concern and attention if they are to become *faits accomplis*. Every one of these goals serves a certain group of supporters as the supreme cause to which they devote their energy and intellect. The mere name of an ardent champion is enough to suggest the cause which that person promotes: Spock means "anti-draft"; Russell means "ban the bomb"; Brown means "black power"; Buck means "concern for American war orphans"; and so on.

In this same way, the mention of the name Christian ought to mean "Kingdom of God"! This is the prime cause for the Christian and Jesus was its supreme revolutionary. The disciple must be willing to place every other social issue or goal further down on his roster of allegiances. If we have believed, we are under orders to make the Kingdom of God our primary cause. Jesus said: "Seek ye *first* the Kingdom of God and all these other things will be given to you!"

There have been times in history when God's Kingdom was quite a fashionable cause and the adherents to it were automatically accorded respect and dignity. Things now are different, however; those who seek a cause with status and respect would probably not mention the Kingdom of God till far down the list.

There is a certain order of status among the various popular causes of our time. A night or two with the network news, David Susskind, or Mike Wallace will reveal our passionate idealisms. Some are militantly working for Black Power. Some are raving over injustice in the ghettos. Some are belligerent doves, others more pacific hawks. There are the open-housing champions, the better-pay-for-teachers knights, and the social rejectionists.

Exposure to mass communication has given us ample opportunity to judge which of these causes is the more worthy or has the best status. It may be more stylish to be a cheerleader in the "anti-war section" than in the "save-the-redwood section." "Justice-in-the-ghetto" may be more pressing as a cause than Bangladesh.

Generally speaking, those causes which have to do with human freedom and justice are the most respected, and this is as it should be. A man with deep sensitivity of soul can empathize with the Czechs who demonstrate under political duress in the hope of gaining new freedom. Any real Christian will loathe the grudging with which liberties have been reluctantly extended to blacks in our country. Human liberty, justice, and happiness should be the causes with the highest status.

All of the really great revolutions of time have been to set men free. That is why Spartacus came with his army of slaves. That is why Moses cried before Pharaoh, "Let my people go." That is why the American colonists returned fire at Concord, why the students revolted against the Czar in 1914, and why Castro marched on Batista. Every one of these revolutions, even those which later betrayed their purposes and dreams, was fired by the desire for greater liberty.

The Scriptures ought to be at the top of the pile as a reference book on the universal human need of freedom. It is the tale of revolutions and freedom. The first books of the Bible contain the story of a man who was a builder of Egyptian cities. As the cities were built with slave labor, Moses listened to old men groan and pant in the brick pits and strong young men cry when they were flogged. While Moses made the cities, God made Moses a revolutionary who vowed that never again would a Hebrew baby be born as chattel for the state's auction block.

Jesus in every sense was a revolutionary interested in human freedom. Isaiah said of the Christ figure, seven centuries before he came:

> The Spirit of the Lord God is upon me, because the Lord hath anointed me to preach good tidings unto the meek; he hath sent me to bind up the brokenhearted, to proclaim liberty to the captives, and the opening of the prison to them that are bound.
>
> —Isaiah 61:1

When Christ did come his whole emphasis was one of complete and utter freedom. Looking out over a world blighted by dishonesty and fettered by immorality and war, he stood and cried in the marketplace, "You shall know the truth and the truth shall make you free." He called for allegiance to his cause: "Go ye into all the world and preach the good news to every creature." Isaiah put simply the entire message of Jesus' revolution: "Go, proclaim liberty!"

Jesus' revolution was one which would employ love and passive resistance, but real resistance nevertheless. His followers had to contend against injustice, prejudice, and war; but they were to do it passively and in love even with their enemies. Here is how you resist and revolutionize the world, said Jesus:

> And if any man will sue thee at the law, and take away thy coat, let him have thy cloke also.
> And whosoever shall compel thee to go a mile, go with him twain.
>
> —Matthew 5:40–41

On another occasion he said bluntly that arms were not the method of the new cause: "Put up your sword; they that live by the sword shall die by it." Christ was a liberator! He was a nonviolent revolutionary advocating the overthrow of ignorance, superstition, hatred, war, and all of the very things that are giving us such trouble twenty centuries later.

One immediate and obvious difference between Jesus as a rebel and these newer rebels is the "ergo" in his thinking. Jesus said in effect: "This is what is wrong in our world; ergo, this is my proposal!" Jesus followed his therefore by a practical suggestion that the subtle turning to the light would produce the answer to the issue. Conversion was the prescription for the ailing world. Jesus knew that to change society, you had to change its constituency person by person. But once this was accomplished, the outcome would not only be right individuals, but right systems and right institutions. That is why he followed his diagnosis with an ergo—a "here's-what-we-do-now."

The new revolutionaries many times, however, have decried the ugliness of what is without saying therefore. For the most part we are aware of what they have told us—something is wrong with the establishment. Accepting that premise, we have waited for their proposals and the proposals have never come. When, as their contemporaries, we asked with concern, "What shall we do?" these young revolutionaries began chanting and throwing fire-bombs and bags of cows' blood. As the police came to protect our property, riots followed. Ill will grew between the upholders of our statutes and the dissenters, but seldom has there come an "ergo"!

An essayist for *Time* magazine wrote an article whose very title is the illustration of what is lacking in modern revolutions. It was called "The Right to Dissent and the Duty to Answer." In the essay was this statement among others:

Demonstrators who . . . urge the world in general to "make love, not war," are indulging in dissent for dissent's sake. They are staging a mindless happening devoid of rational ideas. . . .

. . . Dissent is empty without the suggestion of practical alternatives. Candid answers and explanations are required from the policy makers who must make the decisions.[1]

The fever for reform without solutions is reminiscent of a parable Jesus once told of a house which was cleansed of devils. Nothing was put back into the vacant house and soon it was host to a greater crowd of devils than it had been before. It is relatively easy to spot these devils and with effort to eliminate them. But if the system they inhabit is not made full without them, it will not be long until other devils return to plague the exorcist with new problems.

The dissidents who seem so united when they march in column and file with their sloganized placards demanding some change would splinter into quarreling cells if suddenly their objective was reached and the old system discarded. Though they are lobbying for reform, they have never discussed together what they would do beyond the immediate change for which they clamor. They could never be as whole-hearted in building a new system as they have been in protesting the status quo. While their revolution may have a soul of sorts, it never has had a mind. It does not know how to say, "Therefore"!

Another problem besides the small mind is that of the enlarged heart. The modern revolutionaries have often come talking of love, which seems commendable; yet they have spoken of love with a kind of spongy and gelatinous structure. They have not asked us to love specifics; they have asked us to love utopian platitudes, universal concepts, and complex idealism. Like children, they speak with superlatives when it comes to their emotions. We expect to hear children say, "I love mommy," "I love ice-cream," "I love my teacher," "I love the Staten Island Ferry," etc. But anyone who assesses their real feeling can see that their "love" for everything and everybody is neither mature nor discretionary nor studied. It is doubtful that the generalized love concepts of the rebels really will be specific enough to be of help in the long run.

On the other hand, Jesus taught a specific kind of love which would change the world. It was localized and manageable: "Thou shalt love the Lord with all thy heart and all thy mind and thy neighbor as thyself." His was an exacting requirement, but it was a specific love, firm enough to shape interpersonal disregard into working relationships.

Going beyond the large heart and the small minds of the modern revolutionaries, another flaw of cause becomes obvious—they all seem so transient and short-lived. The critical issues of two years ago have already faded. The paramount social issues "way back then" (24 months ago) are as irrelevant as Stonehenge. A thousand campus charters for yesterday's burning issues are already defunct.

The editor of *Decision* magazine pointed out in a letter to a student protester the transience both of the cause and the rebel. He wrote:

> Dear Mark:
>
> We're very sorry that you got yourself into trouble with the law. . . . Your wish to see the world made more fit for humanity is shared by many, many people, Christians included. We can think of a dozen philosophers, from Plato to Marx, who in times past designed elaborate schemes they hoped would bring about an ideal society.
>
> What's more, by the time six more presidential terms have passed, and you are 44 years old, there will no doubt be another generation coming along with still another plan. Have you in your confinement, ever mused about this possibility? For then you will be a part of the "establishment" and impatient "students for a democratic society" will be on your doorstep, perhaps threatening you and demanding that you yield up your power.[2]

There are dozens of organizations, like the Berkeley Free Speech Movement, which yesterday were burning with zeal but whose voices today are scattered. They are afflicted by a kind of laryngitis that overtakes a movement when it senses that everyone is bored with its posters and slogans.

By way of contrast, the Kingdom of God has been a vital issue for every age, and in two thousand years such tenets as "Come unto me all ye who labor," "Repent and be baptised," "Go ye . . . and preach the good news," have found an

amazing number of supporters in every segment of man's
past. It seems new, forever young, and urgent! Just the same,
there are those who say, even while they admit that it has
been longer-lived than most issues, that at last the Kingdom
is a doddering and senile old cause which will soon be laid
away in the stainless steel archives of tomorrow.

The question of whether or not Christianity really is
passé, like many other questions, will be answered only by
the moving of the years. Christians, however, must believe
that it is a perpetual cause—indestructible, immortal, durable
as the universe itself. The disciple must know that Jesus
Christ really is the "same yesterday, today, and for eternity."
The follower of Jesus of Nazareth must affirm that while
Christianity is two millennia of age, it is not old; rather it has
barely begun its movement into an unending future of undiscovered eternities. This forever new Christianity is main-
tained by a kind of spiritual relativity in which the energy of
the cause is related to the vastness and the timelessness of
God himself.

It is true that no person's life will have greater meaning
than the causes to which he gives himself. Victor Frankl,
who stated that the "will to meaning" is the most basic of
human drives, said of the importance of the cause in the
search for meaning:

> It is my conviction that man should not, indeed cannot,
> struggle for identity in a direct way; rather, he finds identity
> to the extent which he commits himself to something beyond
> himself, to a cause greater than himself. No one has put it
> as cogently as Karl Jaspers: "What man is, he ultimately
> becomes through the cause which he has made his own." [3]

Everyone has a "cause" need. Usually the cause embraced
will demand a rebellion of some kind—political, ideological,
moral, spiritual or other. If it takes a cause to bring meaning
to living, we may also say that the greatest meaning can only
come as we embrace the greater causes.

Warriors who battle for shallow causes will grow tired and

fall away. Their cause and their meaning, perhaps even their desire to live, will all vanish at the same time. And every person who fails to find the proper cause will eventually arrive at the same experience.

Is Christ or his church the proper cause? Opinion is divided. A college student recently said to me, rather point blank, "The church makes me sick!" Reluctantly, I had to confess, that generally it makes me sick too, when it makes great claims and takes few actions. On the other hand, the rapid-growing Jesus movement is irrefutable testimony to the power of his cause.

The zeal of the new revolutionaries is something to marvel at. Their apparent eagerness to suffer for the cause is like the appetite for persecution that once existed among the Christians in the church. Ignatius, an early bishop, is reported to have been blissfully happy on his way to Rome to be martyred. He expressed his drive to die for Christ this way: "I am going to become meal for the bread of God ground between the teeth of lions." Paul of Tarsus said, ". . . I am ready not only to be bound but also to die at Jerusalem, for the name of the Lord Jesus" (Acts 21:13). In *Androcles and the Lion* George Bernard Shaw, admittedly a religious cynic, nevertheless characterized the complex well when he pictured the doomed Christians marching to their death singing (to the tune of "Onward Christian Soldiers"), "Feed us to the lions, we will be devoured."

Similarly in modern movements, to be jailed, fined, or bullied by policemen is the way to be a better man in the revolution. Paul of Tarsus listed the woes he had endured for his cause: "Five times received I forty stripes save one. Thrice was I beaten with rods, once was I stoned, thrice I suffered shipwreck, a night and a day I have been in the deep" (2 Cor. 11:24–25). The apostles of social revolution today would say: "I was bullied by the cops three times, mauled by troopers once, gassed by the National Guard, hailed before the district court and fined," etc., etc.

To the pietist, **it would** seem unfair to compare Paul's

suffering for Christianity to a modern martyr's suffering for draft evasion. One must admit, however, that the motives and drive are similar. Perhaps the analogy points to another truth—that a movement is its most vigorous when it has many martyrs. Christianity's most rapid advances were made in eras of oppression and persecution. Christ himself was a martyr, as were nearly all of his followers in the initial decades of the cause. Now that Christianity is established, the concept of suffering for his cause is more on the order of a toothache. "Carrying our cross" for the Master generally means sitting through an unbelievably dull sermon and smiling in the pain of it, or being sniggered at because of some moral inhibitions relating to the cause.

There is a kind of romance in suffering that gives appeal to an unaccepted cause. But when it finally is received, the suffering and the romance disappear and the mood of the movement settles down, sates itself in victory, and becomes sluggish and fat with indulgences. Its vibrant enthusiasm degenerates into quarrels between its liberal and conservative poles and what once was something to really die for becomes hardly worth the living for.

This may be Christianity's misfortune. The church's apathy has engendered mass nausea. In a burning world, the cause-hungry crowd desperately wants us to do something more vital than debate Calvinism and publish Sunday school papers. In the chaos of a thousand revolutions all going on at once, the critics are saying, "For God's sake, get enrolled in one of them."

Karl Barth summed up the unappealing church in a direct way. Weary with the way the confessing church in Germany had shut its eyes to the plight of the Jews, he warned:

> The real danger and the worst enemy of the confessing church today is the army of neutrals in that non-confessing church which is not yet prepared for any compromise, i.e., the army of those whose symbol consists of two thick blinkers and whose ecclesiastical desire is to be dangerous to no one, and thus letting themselves be in no danger, who to

further this aim, are never at a loss for any possible pa-
triotic, pious and learned argument and who above all have
on their side the powers. . . .[4]

The worst enemies of the church today are the apathetic.
These have lent credence to the prevailing world view that
the church is emaciated and unimportant, valuable only because of its antique filigree and quaint liturgy.

The apathy inside the church is disheartening, and the
clamor of a thousand causes outside the church is maddening.
But Jesus has given us the ultimate cause. It is quieter,
more subtle than the new drives. It does not suffer the panic
inherent in temporal systems when they run out of breath.
It is journalistic. Its story is amazingly simple, whisper clear,
and powerful as thunder. It first arrests the attention of earthlings through the angels: "Peace on earth to men of good
will." Even to men who loudly insist that there are no angels
or demons, it seems a goal worth pursuing. The glass façade
of the United Nations Building, built by men of good will, is
testimony to the angelic wisdom.

The problem is that these men of good will are also men
of self-will. And it is self-will, a synonym for sin and greed,
that has sent us to the brink of cosmicide. The angels had a
solution for that too: "For unto you is born this day in the
city of David a Saviour, which is Christ the Lord." Christ has
come to save us from our own self-will. This is the gospel,
the good news—man can be saved. He needs to be, for the
result of individual self-will is eternal loss, and the result of
national self-will is annihilation.

So Jesus came with an apolitical nation—the Kingdom of
God. To any who enlisted through faith he gave the commission: Tell the good news—there is salvation from self-
will and the death which always follows it.

To save men from their own passions and drives is a battle
that has been going on for these many centuries, but it is
still the primary cause at work in his world. It does not get
the TV coverage that the anti-drafters, the anti-blacks, the

anti-whiteys, and all the other antis get, and therefore, we forget its urgency. Still, we know that while there are no shortcuts to utopia, it can never come without a universal concept of the Fatherhood of God, and the Saviorhood of Christ. When these concepts have been achieved, then and then only shall we have the brotherhood of man.

7 *Space Faith*

Father, thank you for letting me fly this flight. Thank you for the privilege of being able to be in this position; to be up in this wondrous place, seeing all these startling, wonderful things you have created.

Astronaut Leroy Gordon Cooper
Prayer from the *Faith 7* capsule, 1963

SPUTNIK ONE did not roar; it beeped. The rocket which lifted it roared, but when its roaring had consumed all its fuel, it fell dead and silent. Only the beep was heard. But beep it did; not loudly, but constantly, till all the world had heard its monotonous boast in its mindless beeps. Most people were not impressed by its one-word lunacy; they wanted to know what kept it there orbiting like a ping-pong ball at the end of a string, round and round the earth a thousand times over. We were told that Sputnik One was the helpless victim of two vectors: one which kept it moving off into space away from the world, and the other a gravitational attachment that kept it always falling toward its home planet. Hence it flew orbit after orbit.

Its Russian creators had named the odd spheroid Fellow Traveler. It was a fitting name, for it traveled along with the earth, literally running circles around it as the earth traveled its ancient orbit unwaveringly around the sun. This

new satellite joined the old satellite—the moon—that God had
put there ages ago. Man's little moon was not as large as
God's moon, nor was it as romantic; it was a great deal more
talkative, though, even if what it said was uninteresting. But
it was man's moon. Man, the terrestrian put on the planet by
the Creator, was now looking into the night sky and seeing
a part of himself in the majestic infinity that had formerly
been "off limits."

It was perhaps an odd twist of technology that allowed
the first satellite to be the genius of a nation which was so
stubbornly doctrinaire about being atheist. In its own country
all the credit for the orbiting "beepster" was given to the
company of physicists and technicians which had accomplished the marvel. But even if God did not get honorable
mention, it was a great day and an exciting achievement.

The launch of the Sputnik One marked with enthusiasm a
new era in man's fascination with the skies. For centuries he
had studied the stars, measured their movement, used them
in his guidance systems, collected them in constellations, and
through astrology even got them thoroughly involved in the
affairs of men. But they were too distant; he wanted to know
them closer. Perhaps this was part of the naïve legerdemain
of those men in Genesis 11:4 who said, "Come let us build
. . . a tower whose top may reach unto heaven." The tower
never brought the heavens closer; the telescope did, and
rocketry now has placed men in space.

Throughout history there have always been men who
insisted that God disapproved the efforts of the adventurous
to expand the boundaries of their world. Today we must
answer technology's newest hecklers, "Is God anti-space-
exploration?" Or, as some ultraconservative might put it,
"Would Jesus have been an astronaut?" To answer the last
question first, biblical tradition has already made it obvious
that Jesus was from some other realm, a concept which has a
purely spiritual understanding, of course. Nevertheless,
Jesus did come to this world from beyond it. While this does
not say that Jesus would have been an astronaut, it does say

that he was not as earthbound as some of his followers would make him out to be.

Why must anyone assume that because God is for faith, he is always against expanding human experience? God is not against man's learning anything, least of all space. Rather, it seems that God created man with a hunger to know all that he might. It would seem that God dangled before man's wondering eyes a million stars to tempt him first to astrology and then to telescopes and on into exploration. That drive in man to know is God calling him, luring him, tempting him with the undiscovered.

In his autobiography, *Report to Greco*, Nikos Kazantzakis called man's allurement to know, the Cry.

> Blowing through heaven and earth, and in our hearts and the heart of every living thing, is a gigantic breath—a great Cry—which we call God. Plant life wished to continue its motionless sleep next to stagnant waters, but the Cry leaped up within it and violently shook its roots: "Away, let go of the earth, walk!" . . .
>
> "I don't want to. . . ."
>
> But the Cry, without pity, kept shaking its roots and shouting, "Away, let go of the earth, walk!"
>
> It shouted in this way for thousands of years; and lo! as a result of desire and struggle, life escaped the motionless tree and was liberated.
>
> Animals appeared—worms—making themselves at home in water and mud. "We're just fine," they said. "We have peace and security; we're not budging!"
>
> But the terrible Cry hammered itself pitilessly into their loins. "Leave the mud, stand up, give birth to your betters!"
>
> "We don't want to! We can't!"
>
> "You can't, but I can. Stand up!"
>
> And lo! After thousands of eons, man emerged, trembling on his still unsolid legs.[1]

Whether or not we agree with all that Mr. Kazantzakis says, we must admit that the constant drive in humankind to reach further and be more is of God. Not content with the horse and carriage, man designed the automobile. Plagued by his fascination with birds, the same drive in him produced the airplane. Now it is pointing silver darts at infinity, and liquid nitrogen and kerosene are hurling them toward the unknown that must be known.

Gordon H. Clark stated what ought to be the Christian's understanding of our new space age:

> God's first command to Adam contained the injunction to subdue nature. Shooting the moon, therefore, is a divinely appointed task. Unfortunately, however, the ungodly are generally reputed to have obeyed this commandment more successfully than devout Christians have.[2]

If we are to carry out fully God's injunction to Adam to subdue nature, we shall have to admit that all those orbs and bodies and swirling gasses were made by him, too, and are a part of his created nature. Such a concept will make for a big, big God whose immensity may well overwhelm us.

If at the same time, however, we can believe God as infinitely vast as his universe, then we can make friends of faith and space exploration. If it is all his, then discovering Mars will be no more an intrusion of God's domain than was Columbus's discovery of this hemisphere which is also God's. Indeed, not to relate God to space is to make him a terrestrian. In the total dimension of the universe, Earth is an indistinct speck, and to make God an earthling is not only to diminish his size but to negate his universal importance.

The Old Testament writers, at least its later writers, had a view of God as sovereign over the universe. Admittedly, their understanding of the universe was packaged rather small, but God was throughout it all. The psalmist said, "The heavens declare the glory of God, and the firmament showeth his handiwork. Day unto day uttereth speech, and night unto night showeth knowledge. There is no speech nor language, where their voice is not heard. Their line is gone out through all the earth, and their works to the end of the world. In them hath he set a tabernacle for the sun. . . . His going forth is from the end of the heavens" (Psa. 19:1–6). Amos had further written in his book that the Children of Israel ought to seek God, who "maketh the Pleiades and Orion" (Amos 5:8)!

Ethelbert Stauffer demonstrates in a unique way the astrological significance of such an event as the Star of Bethlehem. He says that the star may have been the apparent conjunction of the orbits of Saturn and Jupiter which occurred in 7 B.C. This astronomical event occurs only once every 794 years and would have had the appearance of a more brilliant star than either of the two planets seen singly. He conjectures, however, that it was not only the appearance of this phenomenon which brought the Wise Men to Bethlehem. It was rather the astrology of the conjunction which drew them, for Jupiter was regarded as the star of the universal ruler, and, in the East, Saturn was regarded to be the planet of Palestine. The constellation Pisces in which the conjunction occurred was the star group which symbolized the latter days. When all these data were assembled by these star-gazers, it could only mean that the Universal King of the Last Days had been born in Palestine.[3]

Whether or not this is the true explanation of the Star of Bethlehem is irrelevant to our discussion. It does help to show the sovereignty of God over stars and human events. It is good, of course, that we have lost the superstitions that always accompanied astrology, but it is unfortunate that we have lost the concept of the vast God involved in the universe and in the affairs of individual men.

Space exploration in itself will neither confirm nor abrogate God. Those in whose lives there is already a God concept will have that concept strengthened in contemplating the beyond. Those who do not believe in God will scarcely be converted by a confrontation with the limitless vacuum. These ideas were borne out in two of our primitive space efforts; one an American effort, the other Soviet. When the Russian cosmonaut Yuri Gagarin was hurtling through space on his shallow earth orbit, he confirmed exactly what he had believed before his trip; he had seen space, a dozen sunrises and as many dusks in a single day, but he had not seen God. On the other hand, John Glenn reported that he had been awed by the majesty of God's incalculable creative activity; everywhere he could see God.

In a system where God is not a factor any achievement acquires the tenor of human egoism. If lives are lost on the reentry trajectory, there are no requiems or prayers; there is simply the admission we have failed. If, on the other hand, there is a success, then it may become a glorious opportunity for national narcissism in which men laud men. In such a moment the Russian cosmonaut Gagarin beamed excitedly back from space, "I am an eagle."

Hyper-humanism, a prominent feature of such atheistic space efforts, is always accompanied by an impersonal cosmogony. Natural law, by which any scientific experiment may be calculated, is simply there without the necessity of a God to explain both its presence and its constancy. It is enough for the atheistic technician to say that earth's gravitational exertion is 32 feet per second per second without saying either that God so created it or that God keeps it constantly at that figure. Any calculation starts with an equation or a formula and not with an assumption that God either makes such formulae possible or guarantees their exactness.

In a more Christian-oriented technology, the formulae work the same way. While most technicians would not get God mixed up in the *pi*s and *mu*s they would likely credit all phenomenal predictability to God's laws. When John Glenn went into his epochal space flight, the cliché of the hour became, "Glenn orbits on God's laws." To many Americans it is God's laws which make possible the National Aeronautics Space and Space Administration.

To further illustrate: When Frank Borman, Jim Lovell, and William Anders were on that first maiden voyage of a manned vehicle to the moon, Houston's Apollo Control asked, "Who is at the controls, if anyone?" Since at that moment they were drifting in the earth's gravitational field, they replied, "Sir Isaac Newton, as much as anyone." But Sir Isaac did not really discover gravity; everyone had always

known it was there. It was one of God's laws to which
Newton assigned some symbols and figures and equations.
In reality what the astronauts were saying was that Natural
Law was driving, and in the Western understanding of that
concept it would of course begin with the capital letters. All
Christians would recognize God's sovereignty and his laws
by which either atheists or Christians promote their space
programs.

Dr. Sherwood Wirt of *Decision* magazine, whose influence
in American Christianity is considerable, is one of those who
believe God is anti-space-exploration. In a recent book on
social ethics, Dr. Wirt accepts our "toying with the moon,"
but he considers interplanetary travel not only a waste of
time but actually contrary to the Will of God. His rationale
for his position is that "people aren't made for that. God
wants us to live here on earth until He gives us another
body." [4]

At first glance Dr. Wirt's position would seem to be well
taken—that if God wanted us to visit other planets he would
not have given us a physical system so bound to this earth
with its atmosphere and water and food. The same stand
could be taken against commercial aviation, which lifts two
hundred people at once to a stratum of the atmosphere where
the cold is too severe to endure and the oxygen is too thin for
breathing without pressurization. God did not give us bodies
which could be at home at such altitudes, but it must be
assumed that this area of aviation is not beyond his will.

C. S. Lewis, who did much writing on space and interplanetary travel, did not express this kind of negative attitude. Lewis's only fear was that in making contact with
other inhabited planets we would transmit to them our sin;
and perhaps if they were unable to withstand our invasion
successfully, we might make them victims of our colonial
expansionism.

Some might object to space experiences because they do
seem to chip away at the biblical view of the created order.
For instance, the ancient three-story universe, composed of

hell in the cellar, earth on the mezzanine, and heaven on the
penthouse level, is gone now. We shall have to learn some
new metaphors that express the relationship of these concepts
to the physical universe as it has come to be understood. And
we shall have to translate in the same way the reference in
Revelation 7:1 to the four angels who stand on the four
corners of the earth, for now, having seen pictures of earth,
we know it is round. We shall have to understand that when
Joshua told the sun to stand still he observed that it did
happen. But his command was based on an erroneous assumption that the universe was geocentric. Yet in spite of
the inconvenience that the space age inflicts on our biblical
cosmogony, we may still say the space effort is what God
wants for men.

Several practical reasons exist, in my opinion, that seem to
make it God's will for humankind. First of all, it provides
an area of competition among major nations where supremacy
may be proven without bloodshed and war. This is not to
say that such competition has eliminated the danger and
possibility of war, but it has at least partially diverted
rocketry from its military uses. Surely God must wish for
his world all the peace it can obtain.

The space effort is also providing the world with the
national heroes which our country and others so desperately
need. Ideally, we must try to be like God, but practically we
need some nearer, realistic challenges. When John F. Kennedy introduced Alan Shepard, Jr., after his historic flight,
he humorously quipped:

> We have with us today the nation's number one television
> performer, who I think on last Friday morning secured the
> largest rating of any morning show in recent history. And
> I think it does credit to him that he is associated with such
> a distinguished group of Americans whom we are all glad to
> honor today—his companions in the flight to outer space—
> so I think we'll give them all a hand. They are the tanned
> and healthy ones; the others are Washington employees.[5]

On December 27, 1968, the day of the Apollo 8 splashdown,
Chet Huntley and David Brinkley chatted in their customary

manner, only more excitedly, about the way that the three astronauts involved in that mission had helped fill the long-standing need for a national hero. Surely God must will for us such men to inspire us to be better men.

It may be that God wills our participation in the space effort also because in his plan he wishes for us to eliminate overpopulation and our dwindling supply of natural resources. This concept was expressed by Congressman George P. Miller, chairman of the House Space Committee, when he said:

> The basic unarguable fact is that we are irrevocably committed to exploring space and to sending men out into the stark and hostile vacuum of space for one reason only. That reason is survival, the survival of ourselves and our children as free people.[6]

As colonial expansion brought to Europe's major powers new resources and opportunities for emigration to new lands of opportunity, space may provide a similar hope for our future generations.

God surely wishes for his creatures to continue their quest for understanding and knowledge of creation. Adam's order to subdue nature is the proof-text for those who must have one to support that position. Truthfully, however, the word *subdue* is a little too grand when applied to the universe, for we are a long way from subduing it. But if we cannot subdue it, we may at least analyze it. From recent moon landings we have had a fascinating sampling of the lunar surface to study; each new study brings us closer to a better understanding of how God operated in creating the universe millions of years past.

It seems easier to relate God and space than it is to relate his Son to this new age. Thousands of questions must soon be answered. Must Christ the God-man be an earthling, or are we to know him to be in every sense as cosmic as his Father? Is the Jesus martyred by the Romans an antiquated Savior too cumbersome in his tunic and toga to be Lord to men in silver pressure suits? Can the Christ roar off into space in a

command module with his disciples? This question came
with a rather graphic answer to me recently.

I was visiting Temple Square in Salt Lake City, when I
caught a glimpse of the timeless Christ who truly is the
"same yesterday, today and forever!" In the uppermost gallery
of the visitors' center is a magnificent copy of the Florentine
Christ. It is elevated on a dais which further heightens the
spell it casts and the authority it commands. The wide and
airy room is filled with murals, done in special blues, which
picture the universe. Surprisingly, Christ does not seem alien
among the whirling orbs and rolling spheres, but instead he
seems to rule over them. Indeed he is the cosmic Christ.

From the time of that ancient Jewish Feast Day, Pente-
cost, when Christ became the indwelling Spirit of God, his
relationship to men became totally intrinsic. He went only
where those who believed in him went, living within them.
The Christian men or women who probe space will take him
with them to the beyond, just as they do wherever they go
here on earth. In the coming noonday genius of space technology, we shall have to cease thinking of God come to earth
in Christ, but God come to the *universe* in Christ. The Christ
of the space age will be more than a terrestrian; he will
move wherever those who believe in him move.

Further, if he tarries in his second coming until space
exploration shall have flourished and interplanetary travel is
a commonplace affair, we shall have to alter our concepts
about that advent too. When Bethlehem means that God
came not just to the world in Jesus Christ, but to the universe,
then it will follow that his second advent will be a coming not
just to the world but the entire universe.

A Christ for the universe, in his love for that entire
universe, commits us to a missionary obligation in space.
Such a hypothesis is, at the moment, of course, highly con-
jectural and theoretical. First of all, it presupposes that there
are intelligent beings on other planets, and that God's plan
of redemption in Jesus Christ has not come to those planets.
It further assumes that those beings will have been created

with a capacity for faith as well as intellect, for without both of these qualities there can be no redemptive mission in this world or any other. And if those beings, though intelligent and capable of faith, are physically unlike earth's men, there may be a severe problem in that the glory of the incarnation for earthlings was that Jesus became a man. Even so, the importance of that event is not altogether that God became one of us, but also that he got involved with all of us. The space Christ may have to become not the God involved with earthlings, but the God as he involves himself totally in his universe.

Those of us who follow Christ are experiencing right now, along with all the rest of the world, the infancy of the exciting space age. The Christ and God's record of him in Scriptures are as relevant today as they have ever been. Our faith and our intrigue with space are not warring inconsistencies which we can harmonize only by clever rationalizations. Christ is the miraculously virgin-born Son of the Creator who not only fashioned infinity, but who also raised his Only-Begotten from the dead so that we might have life. Eternal life and space are both creations of God the Father.

Perhaps the perfect harmony of faith and space was seen on Christmas Eve in 1968 as Frank Borman hurtled in his Apollo 8 spacecraft within sixty miles of the moon. Commander Borman read from the Scriptures and offered prayer a quarter of a million miles from the planet where ancient men of God once wrote the very volume from which he read. While he observed this devotional time, the world spun below him, plagued by starvation, crime, war, and a painful hunger for human meaning.

The devout astronaut was out of the world temporarily. He and those who have followed him are well aware that when men enter space, they do so with the same sin and imperfection they have always possessed. For while it may be possible to take a man out of the world through rocketry and technology, it seems impossible to take the world out of men. Wherever we go, on earth or in space, we will need the same redemption as ever. From across the centuries Christ will say to us, who are awed by our own star treks, "I am come that you might have life and that you might have it more abundantly."

8 The Citian: A Study of Anonymous Man

And when he drew near and saw the city, he wept over it . . .

Luke, the Physician

THE PROPHET Jeremiah wrote an elegy to the most important urban center in his land. Jerusalem, smoldering in the fatigue of defeat, was in ruins—a city in swirling ashes and wounded battlements. To the prophet, she was a gallant lady, ravaged by siege and left wounded on a barren hilltop. He began his Lamentation with a pathetic line: "How lonely the city stands . . ."

If the prophet had lived today, and had surveyed our cities, he would probably have used the same words, "How lonely the cities stand . . ." It is strange that the cities, teeming with four-fifths of the nation's peoples, should seem desolate, yet they do. Even those of us who live in the cities find ourselves mentally alienated from them, working in them but not really willing to call ourselves city-dwellers.

We have rejected the cities. Their darkened streets are unsafe. Their ghettos are unsightly. Their fringes are filled with suspicion and dread. Riots are a threat to commerce and trade. Strikes create unrest, and student extremism results in panic and rifle fire.

Many people have amputated themselves from the un-

85

lovely urban mass. Though they would not go so far as to say that they are rural, they want it clear, at least to themselves, that they are not a part of the city. They have a mental picture of the city as that downtown section where the courthouse, city hall, and the skyscrapers are—where the freeways look like so many tangled ribbons of concrete. But they do not live in that part of town; ergo, they are not city-dwellers.

If you ask this kind of New Yorker where he lives, he may answer, "I live in the Bronx"; a Los Angeles resident might say "Glendale"; a Chicagoan, "Oh, I live out in Oak Park." But none of the three would simply answer New York, Los Angeles, or Chicago. We seem to have a desire to remain urban separatists.

In view of the squeeze with which the city limits embrace us, it is amazing that we have managed this kind of separatism. We are stuffed together in stadiums, poked down subway tubes en masse, laid bumper to frustrated bumper in stalled freeways, and pressed into the madding crowd at air terminals; yet we remain apart and alien. We are not citians.

We resent congestion, but it rarely occurs to us that we are a part of it. Our view of congestion is that it is they, the citians, who congest, not we. We are not of the city, and it has no right to force us with its milling and plodding and packing restrictions. We certainly do wish there were less people, ourselves, of course, excepted.

Congestion in the cities affects our whole view of life. A recently published bumper sticker read: Trouble Parking? Join the Planned Parenthood Association. There are people everywhere, and the individual dwellers of the cities resent the cumbersome phone books with their seven-digit census of their "hometown." Far more important than the annoyance is the threat congestion poses to our health. In Calcutta, which will have a staggering 66 million residents by the end of this century, the starving are already shoveled from the sidewalks each morning.

While the growth rate in America is not that dire a calamity, both the census and the congestion will double by the end of the century. In New Jersey, erroneously called the Garden State, the population density is 807 people per square mile, twice the density of India. On Long Island there are fenced lawn areas called "sump pits"; in an effort to preserve some of the ecological balance, these have been placed at intervals throughout the Island to break the concrete and allow some rain water to run back into the ground.

As the cities stretch out their tentacles along interstate highway systems and waterways, they are gobbling up an indecent amount of space (even in semi-rural Wisconsin they are eating up 150 square miles per year). Although it is unlikely that the S.R.O. sign will have to be hoisted tomorrow, or even next year, city dwellers are already plagued by high-rise congestion and a lack of privacy.

Robert Ardrey, in two significant works, *The Territorial Imperative* and *African Genesis*, states that the primary need of people is a little space they can call their own. Undoubtedly the frustration which has built up in part from the loss of space has been a factor in the present unrest and strife in the high-rise megalopolises of today.

It is a paradox that in a packed culture the city dweller lives a rather isolated life. In spite of the fact that every citian must live terribly close to many other people, he does not really know very many of them. It is of course physically impossible for him to know more than a fraction of all those he meets, but he may simply not want to anyway. In today's world, where knowing and being known by very many can be an annoyance, anonymity is often considered to be an asset rather than a liability.

Names and consequently personhood seem irrelevant in a well-oiled society. Roger Shinn tells of receiving a Christmas card with a name on it which would have been meaningless if under the name had not been written "your milkman." Here is a kind of faithful anonymity in which every other morning there is the proper amount of homogenized, skim, and cheese, but the need has never arisen to communicate.

Dr. Shinn further tells of two men who, although they worked side by side in the same room and talked to each other every day, were not very well acquainted. One day, one of the men took the afternoon off to attend his daughter's wedding; the other took the afternoon off to attend his son's wedding. They were both surprised to meet at the same church.

In many respects modern citians are a part of what David Riesman calls the *Lonely Crowd*. There are people all around us, but not persons. The latter have names and needs; the former are functioning gears in the urban machine.

Another reason that anonymity has became so popular is the citian's fear of intimacy in a mobile society. Some statisticians report that as many as one-fourth of all Americans move every year. It may be easier to remain friendless in the city than to face the separation of saying good-by.

William H. Whyte, Jr., in his book *Organization Man*, illustrates this point with an advertisement for shrubbery. The nursery claimed their bushes could be easily transplanted, the reason being that the bushes were transplanted every year so that they would not develop a deep root system which might be damaged in transplanting. Mr. Whyte goes on to suggest that this is also true of men in the city-society. They must put down a lot of roots, but they must not run any of them too deeply. They may otherwise risk damage to their emotional well-being when they are transplanted by industry or commerce to another part of the nation or world.

Gibson Winter describes modern man's plight succinctly:

> The most virulent poison is created by industrial excessive loneliness. Our way of life uproots people, carrying them upward or downward in the struggle for success. Human bonds are pulverized. Those who cling to family ties are soon left behind in the economic struggle. Those who press forward find themselves cut off from friends and associates. We are the uprooted. We are the producers of things and the servants of machines. We live with things, ideas and prices. We rarely have time to live with people.[1]

Simultaneously with the abandonment of people has come the rise of "what-the-hellism." Without intimacy and friendship, meaningful living lacks motivation. "What-the-hellism" goes under a variety of names and results in a hundred forms of social rejection: hippyism, drug abuse, alcoholism, prostitution, crime, etc.

I cannot presume to offer any statistics to support the correlation between "what-the-hellism" and the distant closeness with which we all operate within the cities. But it seems obvious to me that many who no longer care about the meaning of their lives feel that way because they have consistently discovered themselves alone in a world of people.

Suicide, a near relative of meaninglessness, is the leading single cause of death of persons between the ages of fifteen and fifty years, and there may be as many as two million people living in the United States with a history of at least one unsuccessful suicide attempt. A surprising percentage of these depressing suicide statistics can be directly attributed to lonely and meaningless living in the demanding city.

But self-destruction and the "death-wish" do not belong entirely to the unpopular or the social failures. Novelists, actors, politicians—all have been suicides in recent times. Some suicides seem to have nearly everything going for them. Like Edward Arlington Robinson's "Richard Cory," many an affluent and prestigious man is capable of going home to "put a bullet through his head." Robinson does not give us Cory's suicide note, and we cannot help wondering whether he did it because urban living demanded everything but gave him little in return. Was suicide his way of saying to a remote, depersonalized structure, "What the hell"?

As babies continue to arrive and the life-span is pushed closer to the century mark, urban congestion will, of course, become more intense. The Richard Corys will become increasingly frequent. Despair over riots, cleavages, welfare, sanitation and a host of other concerns may also increase.

But the church can have a special ministry to the city if she will accept it. In fact, we may very well have come to the time when the church must accept the challenge of urban redemption, or else.

But the probability that the church will be playing savior to the city looks distant indeed. The city church in the majority of instances has done what her city members have done, preferring not to think of herself as a citian nor of the city as her province. To the church the city is the downtown college, civic center, and commercial district—the same unspoken view that the citians themselves hold.

Christ, however, came preaching in the cities. Admittedly, the situation was different then, but neither the cities of his day nor his own participation in them were as radically different as we might think. As Jesus' own ministry moved through urban congestion, it was often marked by serious riots or the threat of them. In a storm of protest he was driven from Gadara. At Nazareth he nearly lost his life in the violence that erupted when he spoke at a rural synagogue. On another occasion in Jerusalem the mob tried to stone him. The crucifixion itself grew out of civil unrest, mass pressures, and mob violence.

The fiery and dramatic episodes of Christ's revolutionary ministry were punctuated by his love for people and parties. Leslie Weatherhead has pointed out how often in the New Testament Christ is seen at dinner parties and other social gatherings and how full of humor and wit his statements are. But for years, my view of Christianity was so serious that I deeply resented the Christ who could come to earth in the business of redemption and atonement, and yet be so jolly about it. It seemed to me that the Christ who had such intense concern about the absence of human meaning should have been more grave. Yet he went to Matthew's for dinner and wine. At Cana's wedding reception he made more wine; he ate at Zacchaeus's place and at Simon the leper's; he had lunch with Lazarus of Bethany. Now, however, I understand. The cities of his day needed laughter as desperately as the cities of our own need it too.

The Master went into the cities with salvation and laughter, not criticism and apathy. And his ministry has become our commission: the church is called to sing and dance, to change water into wine, to change cold efficiency into warm conversation, to play down liturgy and play up fellowship, to give as great importance to the coffee cup as it does to the communion chalice.

The importance of laughter and fun in the cities was made clear to me on a recent Sunday night. After an evening worship service, which was sparsely attended and drably enthusiastic, I went with several of the church members to a pizza parlor. Golden draughts of beer with fluffy heads and pizza were on all the tables; the atmosphere resembled a delightful blend of Munich and Naples. Everybody there was taking part in a banjo-ragtime sing-a-long. Soon a score of Sunday night worshippers were joining in the contagious merriment. With fascination I began to watch my fellow Christians. They appeared to be having a marvelous time— though it hurts me to say it, a much better time than they had ever appeared to have in church. Suddenly it occurred to me that this is where Christ would have been: at home with pizza and laughter and sing-a-long. It would have been a part of his ministry to the empty citians. Perhaps the church needs to be set loose with a banjo and a Bible, to bring this kind of fellowship and, above all, personhood, to today's anonymous people.

The church, with Christ at her head, must uphold his principles of individual worth and happiness. There can be little doubt that salvation itself means the literal discovery of personhood. The fact that Christ does not really deal with society as a whole but relates to individuals within it is the reason the church may hold the only key to the problem of anonymous man. It alone can eliminate much of the growing tendency toward Richard Coryism.

Lonely citians have so long brushed shoulders without
dialogue that they may think that God, too, has no taste for
conversation with them. Thus, the church needs to remind
them that Christ has a name—Jesus—and that salvation is
in essence an introduction, a name exchange. "Jesus, this
is John Doe. John, Jesus!" In itself that introduction is the
end of anonymous man.

This is simplistic, of course. Evangelism alone will not
cure all that ails the cities. It must be combined with awareness. Short-sighted Christians must be alert for anyone in
the near crowd who is in need of Christ and his fellowship.
Above all, the Christian witness must not be surprised that
the lonely citian will feel the dearth of laughter and song
far more than the absence of Christ. The "soul-winning"
attack is not the answer; the day of the five-minute convert is
over. The current witness must be willing to love and wait,
for the current man who lacks Christ is no longer buying
hell-protection; he is buying, rather, meaning and enjoyment
in life, the city's scarcer commodities.

Sincere churchmen might begin reclaiming the citians by
pledging to help in some definite area. The Big Brother
organization in nearly every city in filled with anonymous
children who need to discover personhood; so are Boys
Clubs, foster homes, and similar situations. Other lonely
citians live in retirement and convalescent homes, VA hospitals, homes for unwed mothers, rehabilitation centers, etc.

Other excellent places to begin ministering in personhood
are the bars and lounges of the cities. Many of the people
who frequent these places are not so much thirsty as they
are hungry for soul and rapport. Christian men and women
who have learned to abandon their antiseptic views and to
minister at ease in such places have found that their witness
will work there, very well.

Recently in our own city, the daily newspaper ran a feature
article about a hippie who came to personhood in Christ.
His picture before and after his discovery of Christ was
printed on the front page, along with the story of his search

for identity. He had participated in riots, disturbances, pot parties and nearly all of the demonstrations which have become the profile of the city in our time. But his conversion itself was not the reason that he made the front page of the paper. It was rather what happened after he shucked his anonymity and laid aside his irresponsibility. He involved himself immediately in an attempt, concerned but patient, to serve "self-discovery" among the lonely citizens of our city. Everywhere he cared and waited, loved and listened, and said to those he met, "You really matter!" But the urgency of his message did not make him gray with concern. All of that came in the midst of laughter and songs and conversation.

There is a way to deal with the distant closeness in the cities. It is to live Christ's primary teaching to this age that every person is a human being. Though he wept over the cities and their aimless milieu, he did not stop with that. Instead he entered the cities with laughter and self-discovery and left us with the only real cure for anonymous manhood.

Harvey Cox recently wrote a book in which he made it clear that the serpent who tempted Adam and Eve is not responsible for the current secular mess. We are not to leave it to the snake, but we are to be responsible for our world and for the plight of the cities. The church can and must help in many ways: social reform, welfare, park programs, etc. But chief of all must be to hack away at the distant closeness; to minister individuality in large doses to those who have never managed to see themselves apart from the faceless mob.

Nathanael, the apostle, came to Christ in a most unusual way. He had been skeptical of the reports he had heard of Jesus prior to their meeting; when finally they did meet, he was surprised that Jesus already knew his name. "Nathanael, isn't it?" said Jesus to the dumbfounded apostle. "I knew you already, when you were sitting under the fig-tree," Christ continued.

It would be interesting to know what Nathanael was do-

ing under that tree. Was he involved in a meditation on
Nathanael? Who was he? Did he matter? Suddenly there is
Christ with a name for the anonymous man.

We cannot know about Nathanael. But we do know that
at least a part of the city's problem will have been solved
when churchmen are able to manage the introductions:

"Human being no. 765,439, this is Christ." And then to
hear Christ say as he said to Nathanael:

"I know you already."

9 The Straight Man in a Bent World

Bless every humble soul who, in these days of stress and strain, preaches sermons without words.

Peter Marshall
Mister Jones, Meet the Master

THE CATHEDRAL of Notre Dame has mothered Paris for most of a millennium. Her dignity has been overshadowed for some by the grandeur of the city's newer structures— Versailles, the Arch of Triumph, and, of course, the Eiffel tower—but even those who scorn her drab antiquity must admire her steadfastness. She has been around quite a while—much longer than the tourists, the Renaults, Peugeots, and Citroens, the ice-cream vendors, and curio peddlers that all seem constantly to be trying to crowd her off into the Seine.

Upon seeing the cathedral for the first time, I struggled to ignore the cosmopolitan congestion and see it as Victor Hugo must have. Peasants, gypsies, haycarts, alchemists, and priests were part of its medieval silhouette. I tried to see, high in the campanile, the hunchback man who played like a spider on the bell ropes. Do you remember him?— Quasi Modo. He was subintelligent, slack-jawed, and deafened by all of his close work with the huge bells of the cathedral. Nature had dealt with him in a grotesque way. He was bent by an indescribably ugly knoll of sinew and bone that sat mockingly upon his athletic frame. He was a bent man in a straight world, an object alone and to be pitied.

Hugo's novel is a spellbinding contrast of a bent man in a straight society. But a millennium before Notre Dame raised her proud head on the Ile de Cité, there was born in a Roman province a man who was not deformed, and who insisted the world was bent and he was straight. He called himself God's Son—God's straight man for a bent world. The world's deformity was caused by immorality and greed and war: in short, sin. Christ did not believe that it was hopelessly bent—he thought it might be straightened, but only as man by man the deformity was erased.

The only way that bent people could ever be straight was first by trying to make their lives like that of the Son of God. Only as they took him for their commander and worshipped him as their ideal would they ever be straight. He was to be the plumb line by which every man measured his own rectitude. He was a statue of dignity in a land of dwarfs, but in some sense he was the pattern, and men who imitated him would restore the fuller dignity of the image of God to the world.

One would think that this pattern for moral uprightness would have inspired the whole world into an immediate attempt at rightness, truth, and liberty. Still, here we are twenty centuries later, not much like him, and perhaps not wanting much to be like him though in some few respects we human gnomes have begun to resemble the ideal God gave in Christ. Hospitals, orphanages, schools, welfare programs, and various kinds of social suffrage make it clear that we have gained a little of the stature he idealized. But war, discrimination, genocide all constantly remind us that we still are gnomes—the curiously deformed images of God, not yet erect as is our example. Why is this so?

God's Adam has always found some substitute ideal, a second-rate image, and has then proceeded to make himself in that inferior fashion. Men have made it painfully obvious that they would rather be like men than like God. They will throng the tyrant and ignore the Christ. They will follow a Charles Martel, a Genghis Khan, a Caesar, a Napoleon, or a Castro. All of human history is the story of men's allegiance to men. God looks down with emptiness on the junkyard they have made of his world; a junkyard filled with dented armor, broken political systems, tattered and threadbare causes. No generation ever looks out on the junkyard and says, "I'll follow God!" Each new age rather searches for some new evangelist of social salvation, then goes the same way as all others.

It does not matter that these human redeemers are despotic; they will be adored, sometimes by the entire world. A German prayer during Hitler's regime went this way:

> Thou, O God, hast given us Adolf Hitler as our leader, that he may bring us freedom and our daily bread, and that he may lead us through labor to see and to fulfill Thy service. Lord, rule over us through Adolf Hitler, and bless him with Thy light and Thy strength.[1]

The decade which followed that prayer showed the world what can happen when men follow men. It is impossible for the crooked men to straighten out the world when they follow a crooked man; their efforts always end in a deep tangle of frustration and death. This then is the reason that God gave us Christ, the straight one, the pattern for the crippled world.

Unfortunately, our era, like the rest, is trying to straighten it all out by other means. Well-meaning souls have gathered in half a million camps fighting half a million problems. Some are trying to straighten the world by cleansing the ghetto. Others are bending their efforts in an attempt to stop wars. Here and there are the militants who are trying to start wars in a beachhead against prejudice.

Many of these "knights" have been the nation's pastors. Most of them are sincere in wanting to help, and many have made their crusade to correct some social ill an auxiliary part of the Kingdom of God. Other pastors have merely replaced the Kingdom of God with their particular cause, and spend themselves eagerly in its behalf. Some ministers have never tried to relate the two, ignoring completely one or the other.

Victor Frankl, it seems to me, is right when he says that the basic human drive is the "will to meaning." It follows that the meaning one has in life derives largely from the cause or causes which he embraces. As God's fifth column in his deformed world, we must be careful that we do not abandon priorities and pick up some fifth-rate banner. The minister particularly must not tilt at mills; he must be the big thinker. His calling is to imitate the man of Nazareth and not the man of La Mancha.

How can we help our bent world? We must practice two concepts which, first considered, seem opposite and unreconcilable: we must be willing to withdraw ourselves and be separate from our world, but, conversely, we must have the courage to penetrate it. Both of these avenues are lined with critics.

Looking at Jesus and John the Baptist will serve to illustrate. John was a recluse—a monk, a hermit. He scorned the gayer life of the cities and spent his years, short as they were, in eroded washes and canyons of the Jordan, lonely and apart. Jesus, on the other hand, went where the action was. He came preaching in the cities, Decapolis, Jerusalem, Jericho. He went to weddings and dinner parties. He did not traffic in sin but he trafficked with sinners.

Both Jesus and John received harsh criticism. John was criticized for his asceticism. People said that John "had a devil." He would have to be crazy, they reasoned, to stalk around the Jordan jungles in haircloth, munching grasshoppers. Of Jesus they said, "Look, he is a gourmand and an alcoholic!" If neither Jesus nor John the Baptist could escape criticism for these two principles, we must expect to receive it also.

We are to love the world and continue Christ's strategy for saving it. Like John we must avoid being chummy with it. We must never love the world supremely: remember Lot's wife? Paul counsels us, "Come out from among them and be ye separate!" But at the same time this cannot be a proof-text for monasticism. We are not to live wholly apart. Our living is to be tangential to God's world, but not imbedded in it.

In some ways the commandment to be separate seems unfair. After all, we are sinners and we cannot help it. We arrived on earth with a tendency toward sin. God seems to have created us black and then demanded that we be white. After putting us here quite naturally he has then demanded that we become supernatural.

The biblical suggestion that we are "ambassadors for Christ" means that we are on duty in a foreign, alien world, representing a better one. That being true, we must not identify with the world where we serve but with the one from which we are sent.

This very thing is the major reason for the slowdown in our attempt to redeem the broken world. We have come from the embassy, talking about the better way, but so thoroughly immersed in the common things that no one has taken us seriously. We talk about a world free from vices, while all the time we indulge in every sort of vice, chemical and moral. Somewhere must come the great divorce from our milieu.

It may seem to the reader that I am as Victorian as a velvet settee. But I am bothered that "Christians" seem to feel no compulsion to live separately, and therefore redemptively, in this world. There is often no fundamental difference between the "Christian" and the uncommitted as far as their affairs can be observed. The superior virtue Christians claim is simply not apparent.

Instead of demonstrating our stand against immorality, we modify our mores until they coincide with those of the aliens. We paganize the faith so that we can be comfortable and more acceptable to the bent people. We mold our convictions so that they do not have any rough unpolished edges that might barb the terrestrians.

Perhaps there was a time when we took this separation thing a bit far. For instance, when I was a child, the church condemned all movies, for they were a corruptive influence on young minds. Simply put, they were "of the devil"! Even Hopalong Cassiday, my hero to adolescence, was a sinner. When this idea was first presented to me, I was struck with unbelief that the church would condemn him with all the rest. Good, old milk-drinking, never-shoot-'em-in-the-back Hopalong a sinner? Never!

Similarly, we lashed out at jitterbugging, playing cards, and snuff. Admittedly, we may have been falling over on our backs to keep from falling on our faces. But look at the permissiveness that the Christian world has granted itself in these later days. Fewer than three percent of the movies released in a single recent year were open and recommended to children. In the same year we spent one billion dollars more on movies than we had ever spent to curb crime and violence in the nation's cities. And of course right in the middle of the theater-goers are the "Christians."

They are also in the queue to buy the pornography on the newsstands. They are consuming an unbelievable amount of liquor even for Americans. Home life is dissolving. Drug abuse is unbelievably common. These are the rather ordinary pastimes of some of the "new disciples," who shrug off all their indulgences as inconsequential while sin is literally bending the world into chaos.

Remember Jesus' third temptation in the wilderness. It was the devil with a globe in his hand, enticing Jesus with the world. "It is yours if you want it," he taunted. Jesus refused it, but we do not. Satan still stands before Christ's disciples and tempts them with the globe, whereupon they chuck the Kingdom of God and embrace the world. Loving it as we do, we shall never redeem it. Like a dry sponge, worldliness will absorb the entire Kingdom of God until all the good news has been digested in secularism.

The Kingdom of God comes to rack at about the same rate that the Christian loses his aloofness in his affair with the world. No believer may be committed fervently both to his God and his indulgences. He will be as large or as small as the things which he pursues.

We are in essence what we experience. The man who reads pulp will not think with the dignity of a Shakespeare. The person who consistently sees dirty entertainment will become that kind of person. We are the sum of all our indulgences.

> It's a very odd thing—
> As odd as can be—
> That whatever Miss T. eats,
> Turns into Miss T.

What we take into our minds and hearts becomes a real part of us from which we can never really separate ourselves.

Further, our indulgences may do more than actually control us; they may destroy us. They may do it to us in such a way that all the while they are gaining the upper hand we still feel ourselves in control. Jack London once wrote concerning his deadly affair with alcoholism:

> Mine is no tale of a reformed drunkard, and I have not reformed. . . . No . . . I shall take my drink on occasion. With all the books on my shelves, with all the thoughts of the thinkers shaded by my particular temperament, I have decided coolly and deliberately that I should continue to do what I have been trained to want to do. I will drink—but, oh, more skillfully, more discreetly than ever before. Never again will I be a peripatetic conflagration.[2]

Three years later, pressed by the indulgences he had "discreetly" allowed himself, he committed suicide.

A too chummy affair with the world may not necessarily destroy us, but it may destroy God for us and for those whom he might otherwise reach through us. At least, it will destroy the redeeming, personal God. Suicide is not the usual end of unseparated living—it is deicide, Christicide. For in our sundry indulgences, we often succeed in slaying the living Redeemer for our spectators.

Will we ever come out of the world long enough for its dwellers to notice there is a difference? It is doubtful, for we have accepted hypocrisy as a more comfortable way to live. We like the claims of Christ, but we would rather leave them unfulfilled than be rejected ourselves. Christ is all right; it's just these damned crosses that we do not like lugging around.

The ideal is to be in the world, but not of the world—to live, but to live separately. Here is the other principle we must honor to participate in God's redemption. When Jesus said, "Let your light so shine before men that they may see your good works and glorify your Father which is in heaven," he meant, Get into the bent world and go straight.

The trick is to live separately without being recluse. No one, for instance, could call Jesus a sinner; yet they could say, "How is it that he eateth and drinketh with publicans and sinners?" (Mark 2:16). Adroitly, Jesus always side-stepped sin but squarely encountered life.

Some have falsely assumed that since Jesus was the Son of God his temptations were paper ones and never really came upon him with any passionate intrigue. Nothing could be farther from truth.

Recently, I visited an amusement park which is so famous for its roller coaster that when anyone asks whether you have been to such and such an amusement park, they literally want to know if you have ridden the roller coaster there. That experience can be a terrifying one, with its spastic turns, plummeting dives, and wailing passengers. Still, you cannot really claim to have been to the amusement park if you by-pass that ride.

Similarly, if Christ is going to be fully man he must be tempted as a man. He does not have to sin to be a man, but he must struggle with it to be a man; he must come

out of the stands and get in the arena with the devil himself
—the same arena where we are born and fight and die.
Unless he has battled in the arena we will not have him shout-
ing down his instructions from the press section, telling us
that although he has never been there he knows how it is to be
done.

In every sense Christ was separate from, yet fully involved
in his world. He had to be. He had come to conquer sin and
that is where the sin was—in the world. He could not conquer
sin from some sterile tower, or some disinfected heaven.

One segment of his church has a more antiseptic hope. To
be sure, they want to see the bent people straightened, but
they want to do it with more clinical methods, which usually
means Bible-under-the-arm visitation and witness. "Pick up
the fallen!" they cry, "but do it with rubber gloves." These
people see sinners as lepers and salvation as gamma globulin,
and of course the only place the diseased may be treated is in
the untainted lysol atmosphere of the church met in worship
and singing, "Just as I am without one germ." It annoys me
that we are so afraid to go out where the bent people live and
to serve the Lord there.

The *General Next to God*, William Booth, came at a time
when English Christians were both Victorian and antiseptic.
This double myopia kept the churchmen rehearsing their
catechism in starched collars in their stately church houses.
While they went through their clinical liturgy a safe distance
from the slums, the general was out in the lifeboats, rescuing
the perishing. It was strange that he alone felt God's love
for the gutter. Through him by the grace of God the ghettos
were set afire with brassy hymns and the salvation the
establishment only mouthed.

There are similarities between Christian practice in Victorian England and church-bound Christianity today. We
pray for the salvation of the people "on the other side of the
tracks," but we would rather they be saved in someone else's
church. We set up a downtown mission to win the un-
desirables, but mostly to keep them downtown. A bus would

be a cheaper way to get them into church, but it would be hard on our suburban status and image. Our women's missionary societies pray for the salvation of the heathen in Tanganyika, but they have never won one person to Christ in their own church. Over tea and brownies they discuss the starving Mongolians, without the slightest twinge of conscience over poverty in their own city. It is tidier to practice our concern for the distant unsaved in the church.

Christ touched every part of his world. Lepers were amazed that he dared to confront their contagion in the name of his Father. A Samaritan woman was stupefied that he would offer her living water, since the "Jews had no dealings with the Samaritans." His disciples were amazed that he had no fear of the Gadarean madman Legion, whose insanity perished in a herd of swine. He loved his Father's world and redeemed all of it that he could, touching it with forgiveness and health.

One can imagine the cleansed leper as he cries on finding himself a whole man, "He touched me!" Filled with awe and health and the joy of knowing that he had been touched by courageous heaven, he could never again be the same man. God had met him, not in the clinic by a hard-won appointment, but rather in the world, and had cleansed him there.

Under her pen name Liz Burns, Gertrude Behanna put the whole concept of Christ in the world in a very warm way. Shortly following her conversion, she was discovered sober at a cocktail party. Since that was not her usual condition at such a gathering, she was obvious merely for her abstinence. It was inevitable that someone would ask her why she wasn't drinking. Someone did, and she proceeded to tell him how she had met God after a suicide attempt and in what an unusual way he had spoken to her. The man was flabbergasted that at a cocktail party someone should be telling him about a God who speaks to people in need. He blurted out, "He speaks?" and Liz answered,

"Yes, he speaks, He speaks just like you and me; that's funny, isn't it? You'd think it would be in Thee's and Thou's

but it isn't. I guess that's so we can understand. Remember
the trial of Joan of Arc? They asked her if God spoke to her
in French, and she said, 'I hear Him in French.' " [3]

What the world needs is to be able to take God to a cocktail
hour and come away with a positive witness—to say even
there, amid the hilarity and the clanging goblets, "He touched
me; he spoke to me not in the Thee's and the Thou's of the
liturgy, but in my language, through some believer who
was not afraid of contamination."

Evangeline Booth was witnessing in the streets to a fallen
woman who seemed untouched by all she was being told.
Sensing that she was not being heard, Evangeline, in concern
for the woman, kissed her. "She kissed me!" cried the poor
woman, suddenly coming to consciousness. Then, turning to
Evangeline, she said, "Talk to me now about a Christ who
can make a woman like you. I am ready to listen." [4]

Here we are in the bent world; it may be far more ready to
listen than we think. Like Christ, we spend most of our lives
eating and drinking with "publicans and sinners." We have
had the opportunity to tell them of him, but we simply have
not used it. Instead of honoring our commitment to help
straighten the bent world, we have slipped clumsily into the
posture of its citizens. They think that our lives are just as
bent as theirs and perhaps they are right.

Our silence at least is treasonous. Knowing the formula for
salvation, we live without compassion in the world of the
damned. We are surgeons who know how to deal with deformity but in our hardness of heart we refuse to use our
knowledge. We accept the bent people exactly as they are
without ever telling them what they might be. We must be
God's straight men, practicing his love at large in the world.
We must let them know that God's love has come to spend
the night of human despair and that he delights in making
poor half-men whole.

Notes

CHAPTER 1

1. William Barclay, *In the Hands of God* (New York: Harper and Row, 1966), pp. 97–98.
2. Gabriel Vahanian, *The Death of God* (New York: George Braziller, Inc., 1957), p. 6.
3. Gibson Winter, *The Suburban Captivity of the Churches* (New York: The Macmillan Company, 1966), p. 167.
4. Roger L. Shinn, *Tangled World* (New York: Charles Scribner's Sons, 1965), p. 156.

CHAPTER 2

1. Henlee H. Barnette, *The New Theology and Morality* (Philadelphia: The Westminster Press, 1967), pp. 92–93.
2. Joseph Sittler, "The Care of the Earth," from *Sermons to Intellectuals*, ed. Franklin H. Littell (New York: The Macmillan Company, 1963), p. 19.
3. William Sloane Coffin, Jr., "Vietnam: A Sermon," in *The Vietnam War: Christian Perspectives*, ed. Michael P. Hamilton (Grand Rapids: William B. Eerdmans Publishing Company, 1967), pp. 69–70.
4. Donald A. Wells, *The War Myth* (New York: Western Publishing Company, Inc., Pegasus, 1967), p. 154.
5. Ibid., p. 147.
6. Ibid., pp. 32–35.
7. Pierre Berton, *The Comfortable Pew* (New York: J. B. Lippincott Company, 1965), pp. 16, 18.
8. Martin Heidegger, *German Existentialism* (New York: Philosophical Library, Inc., 1965), pp. 46–47.

9. Kenneth Scott Latourette, *A History of the Expansion of Christianity*
10. Teilhard de Chardin, *The Phenomenon of Man* (New York: Harper & Row, 1959), pp. 274 ff.

CHAPTER 3

1. Earl H. Brill, *Sex Is Dead* (New York: The Seabury Press, 1967), p. 125.
2. Daniel T. Niles, *That They May Have Life* (New York: Harper & Row, 1951), pp. 63–64.
3. Dietrich Bonhoeffer, *The Cost of Discipleship* (New York: The Macmillan Company, 1949), pp. 49–50.
4. Harvey Cox, *God's Revolution and Man's Responsibility* (Valley Forge, Pa.: The Judson Press, 1965), p. 15.
5. Ibid., p. 31.
6. Paul Scott, "One Human Being to Another," *Guideposts*, December 1968, pp. 12–14.

CHAPTER 4

1. Will Durant, "Man Is Wiser than Any Man," *Reader's Digest*, November 1968, p. 86.
2. Quoted in Norman Vincent Peale, *Sin, Sex and Self-Control* (Greenwich, Conn.: Fawcett Publications, Inc., 1965), p. 65.
3. Evelyn Millis Duvall, *Why Wait Till Marriage?* (New York: Association Press, 1965), p. 11.
4. Ibid., p. 88.
5. Ibid., p. 65.
6. Harvey Cox, *The Secular City* (New York: The Macmillan Company, 1965), p. 200.

CHAPTER 5

1. Albert Camus, *The Fall* (New York: Alfred A. Knopf, 1959), p. 15.
2. Paul Tillich, *The Shaking of the Foundations* (New York: Charles Scribner's Sons, 1948), p. 160.
3. John Osborne, *Luther* (New York: New American Library, 1963), p. 74.
4. Ibid., p. 118.
5. Martha Shipton, "Mother Shipton's Prophecies," *The Best Loved Poems of the American People*, ed. Hazel Felleman (New York: Doubleday & Company, 1936), p. 636.
6. Dietrich Bonhoeffer, *Letters and Papers from Prison* (New York: The Macmillan Company, 1953), p. 162.

7. William Barclay, *Fishers of Men* (Philadelphia: The Westminster Press, 1966), p. 113.
8. Roger Mehl, *Images of Man*, tr. James H. Farley (Richmond, Va.: John Knox Press, 1965), p. 5.

CHAPTER 6

1. *Time* magazine essay, May 12, 1967, p. 23.
2. Sherwood Wirt, *Decision* magazine editorial, "Letter to a Student Protester," September 1968, p. 2.
3. Victor E. Frankl, *Are You Nobody?* (Richmond, Va.: John Knox Press, 1966), pp. 26–27.
4. Karl Barth, *The German Church Conflict* (Richmond, Va.: John Knox Press, 1956), p. 75.

CHAPTER 7

1. Nikos Kazantzakis, *Report to Greco*, as quoted in John A. T. Robinson, *In the End God* (New York: Harper & Row, 1968), pp. 7–8.
2. David E. Kucharsky, "Open Letter to the Apollo 8 Space Men," *Christianity Today*, December 20, 1969, p. 31.
3. Ethelbert Stauffer, *Jesus and His Story* (New York: Alfred A. Knopf, 1959), pp. 32–33.
4. Kucharsky, "Open Letter."
5. Bill Adler, ed., *The Kennedy Wit* (New York: Bantam Books, 1964), p. 86.
6. Kucharsky, "Open Letter."

CHAPTER 8

1. Gibson Winter, *Love and Conflict* (New York: Doubleday & Company, Inc., 1958), p. 183.

CHAPTER 9

1. Martin Heidegger, *German Existentialism*, p. 46.
2. Upton Sinclair, *The Cup of Fury* (Old Tappan, N.J.: Fleming H. Revell Company, 1965), pp. 7–8.
3. Gertrude Behanna, *The Late Liz* (New York: Popular Library, 1957), pp. 179–180.
4. Harold E. Dye, *The Weaver* (Nashville, Tenn.: Broadman Press, 1952), pp. 89–90.